Direction
and Destiny

Direction
and Destiny

MAXIE D. DUNNAM

ABINGDON PRESS
Nashville • New York

DIRECTION AND DESTINY

Copyright © 1967 by Abingdon Press

Library of Congress Catalog Card Number: 67-11005

Scripture quotations designated: Goodspeed are from *The Complete Bible, an American Translation,* by Edgar J. Goodspeed, Copyright, 1939, by the University of Chicago Press; Moffatt are from *The Bible: a New Translation,* Copyright, 1954, by James Moffatt; Phillips are from *The New Testament in Modern English,* Copyright, 1958, by J. B. Phillips; NEB are from *The New English Bible, New Testament,* © the Delegates of the Oxford University Press and the Syndics of the Cambridge University Press 1961 and are reprinted by permission; RSV are from the Revised Standard Version of the Bible, Copyright, 1946 and 1952, by the Division of Christian Education, National Council of Churches. Quotations from *Markings* by Dag Hammarskjöld, trans. by Leif Ajoberg & W. H. Auden, copyright, © 1964 by Alfred A. Knopf, Inc. and Faber & Faber, Ltd., are reprinted by permission of the publishers. Quotations from *To Catch an Angel,* by Robert Russell, are reprinted by permission of Vanguard Press. Quotations from *The Cocktail Party* and "The Hollow Men" from *Collected Poems 1909-1962* by T. S. Eliot are reprinted by permission of Harcourt, Brace & World and Faber and Faber. Quotations from "Mending Wall" from *Complete Poems of Robert Frost,* copyright 1930, 1939 by Holt, Rinehart and Winston, Inc.; copyright © 1958 by Robert Frost; copyright © 1967 by Lester Frost Ballantine; reprinted by permission of Holt, Rinehart and Winston, Inc. "Earth Is Enough" by Edwin Markham is reprinted by permission of Virgil Markham. Quotation from "The Gate of the Year" by M. Louise Haskins is reprinted by permission of Cristy & Moore. Quotation from "A Materialist Pictures Man" is copyright 1957 Christian Century Foundation; reprinted by permission from the October 2, 1957 issue of *The Christian Century.* Quotation from *Procession* by Kahlil Gibran is reprinted by permission of Philosophical Library. Quotation from "The Winds of Fate" by Ella Wheeler Wilcox is reprinted by permission of Rand McNally & Company. Quotation from "Call to Commitment" by Billy Graham is used by permission; © 1960, The Billy Graham Evangelistic Association. Quotation from *Harvey* by Mary Chase, copyright, 1943, 1944, 1953 by Mary Chase; reprinted by permission of Brandt & Brandt.

SET UP, PRINTED, AND BOUND BY THE PARTHENON PRESS AT NASHVILLE, TENNESSEE, UNITED STATES OF AMERICA

With love to Jerry
. . . who helps with directions

PREFACE

D. T. Niles, dynamic leader in the Methodist Church in Ceylon, has defined evangelism as "one beggar telling another beggar where to get bread." Those who would share the joy of coming into, and growing in, the Christian life know the meaning of this. Though they may be still hungry, a source of "bread" has been found, and the beggar can but share it.

This book is an attempt at sharing. Though little *bread* may be found here, perhaps someone who is wandering falteringly will receive some *direction* and move toward his *destiny* as God's child. If this happens, if even a morsel is taken, then this beggar will be happy.

MAXIE D. DUNNAM

CONTENTS

9

DETERMINATION

DISCIPLINE

DEVOTION

DEVELOPMENT

DIVIDENDS

DESTINY

DIRECTION

Looking for New Life?

> "When anyone is united to Christ, there is a new world; the old order has gone, and a new order has already begun."—II Cor. 5:17 NEB

At our house we eat breakfast about nine o'clock in the morning. This doesn't mean at all that our day begins then. My day usually begins about three hours earlier, but this seems to be about the time when the children are sufficiently awake and we can sit down together. My study is at home, and this becomes a convenient arrangement for all concerned.

I must admit that the television has something to do with it. Cartoons begin about seven-thirty, and on the station our children view there is a break at nine o'clock. And what a break! Jack La Lanne comes on at that time. For those whose TVQ is not very high, Jack La Lanne is a physical exercise authority.

For some reason Kim, our six-year-old, likes him. So usually the television stays on while we eat breakfast.

Have you ever tried to eat toast and scrambled eggs to the cadences of "one, two, three, four" and the rhythmic beat of a knee-bend exercise set to music? It's quite an experience!

We sat down one morning just as Hobo Kelly was going off. Then came this melody: "Happy Birthday to You." And there appeared Jack La Lanne with a startling message against the background of that happy birthday tune. "Today," he said, "we want to celebrate your birthday. This can be your real birthday." At that point I began to listen more intently. "You can be born again, today!" he added.

I settled myself with a gulp of orange juice and was ready to listen to the sermon, but in the next sentence discovered that it was not a sermon. He was talking about the new life that could be ours through his program of physical exercise.

My toast was cold and crackly now, but it was worth it. Here was a man convinced that what he had to offer was new life. I went back to my study mumbling, "Old Jack, you don't know the half of it—you ought to hear my message of new life." I picked up the New English Bible and read this fresh translation of II Corinthians 5:17: "When anyone is united to Christ, there is a new world; the old order has gone, and a new order has already begun." I remembered the King James translation, "If any man be in Christ, he is a new creature: old things are passed away; behold, all things are become new." Jack La Lanne didn't have anything on Paul!

My mind started vibrating a bit. Jack La Lanne is not the only man today offering new life. Scores of hucksters offer life-changing wares, and often at a very low price. The marketplace is filled with commodities that claim miraculous powers for the transformation of humanity. The last decade has witnessed a booming business in special health foods all potently geared to give us new life. The hidden persuaders do their jobs well, and the new-life schemes attract more and more.

Sooner or later we learn that new life doesn't come from consumer commodities or easy-life gadgets. It comes from a discovery of spiritual realities and a live relationship with God.

Dag Hammarskjöld has made us richer by leaving his private reflections which he began to jot down when in his early twenties. These have been preserved and published in a book entitled *Markings*. This brilliant and sensitive intellect was fully alive to the main springs of his being. Somewhere along the way he had made a commitment that affected his entire life. He reported it in retrospect: "I don't know Who—or what—put the question, I don't know when it was put. I don't even remember answering. But at some moment I did answer *Yes* to Someone—or Something—and from that hour I was certain that existence is meaningful and that, therefore, my life, in self-surrender, had a goal."

Real meaningfulness comes and a new life is ours when we make this kind of commitment. I knew that morning at breakfast that Paul had a better formula than Jack La Lanne. "If any man be in

Christ, he is a new creature: old things are passed away; behold, all things are become new."

Prayer: We *are* looking for new life, our Father. May this day be the beginning of our discovery of Christ as the source of the new life we need. *Amen.*

One Decision After Another—and a Life Is Built

> "Choose you this day whom ye will serve."
> —Josh. 24:15 KJV

In his autobiography, *To Catch an Angel,* Robert Russell tells the story of his growing blindness:

At six, while the shadowy borders crept closer and closer, finally to engulf me, I slipped quietly into that land where there is no light, where the yellow sunshine no longer lies in pools of liquid gold on polished mahogany, where white lilacs no longer hang like ghostly lamps in a green night. Here the sunshine is warmth, the mahogany smoothness, and the lilac a deep well of fragrance into which one can plunge and drowse away one's life.

But this change of the sun from light to warmth, of the mahogany from color to smoothness, and of the lilac tree next door from whiteness to fragrance, was not dramatic. It was slow, very slow; it took more than a year.

I was too young to be firmly committed to living in a world of light; and so, as I wandered through the land of evening and at last crossed its borders, my ears became accustomed to the darkness, and as my dependence upon them grew, so did their power. So gradually did they accept the function of my eyes that there was no specific time when I knew the change had been completed. There was no crisis. I did not know when I became a citizen of the night.

Is this not the way our lives are built? One decision after another, one experience after another— and our destiny is set. This is more often a subtle, slow process, hardly ever dramatic. Here a choice, there a choice, and the die is cast.

Our tests do not always come up in explicit fashion. They come, and we respond according to the "set" of our lives. One of the moving scenes in Joseph Conrad's *Lord Jim* comes near the close of the story when Jim is seeking to explain how he has come to this point in life when he must quit running, cease surrendering to fear, and face whatever lot he must. "Something happens," he says. "Then you lie about it; then you try to cover it up; then things start moving so fast that you are impelled in a certain direction." Again, this is the way it happens. Gradually, and often unconsciously —certainly without realizing the full import—we move on from one decision to another, and a life is built.

Daily living, then, is serious business. We can't amble carelessly along the road of life foolishly thinking that the way we walk today will have nothing to do with how we go tomorrow. Life has a law that is immutable. We pay tomorrow for our foolishness today. Marital infidelity today means heartbreak tomorrow. Calloused self-centeredness today means loneliness and desolation tomorrow. Cultivation and gratification of only the physical senses today means futility and emptiness tomorrow.

The opposite is true also. A life committed to

17

Christ, invested in meaningful service, disciplined in moral responsibility and spiritual sensitivity, means growth and eventual maturity. It means strength and resources for whatever the future might hold.

Setting the direction of our lives is the most important single thing we can do.

Prayer: We hear thy call, O Christ, "Follow me." This is the direction in which we want to go. Keep us steady as we travel. Amen.

Degrees in Freedom

> "I have put life and death before you . . . choose life, then, that you and your children may live, by loving the Eternal your God."
> —Deut. 30:19-20 Moffatt

All of life is decision. The decisions we make today are dependent upon decisions we made yesterday. The decisions we make tomorrow will be affected by the decisions we make today. Eric Fromm in *From the Heart of Man* has said, "decisions are not made on some final day but early in one's development. Life is a process of degrees in freedom. Most people fail not because they are bad, they fail because they do not wake up to see that sometime at a fork in the road they have to decide. They are not aware when life asks them a question and they still have an alternative answer. With each step along the wrong road it becomes increasingly difficult to admit that they are on the wrong road."

So it is! There are degrees in freedom. Our freedom of decisions is dependent upon the responsible exercising of that freedom at every fork along the road of life.

In T. S. Eliot's play *The Cocktail Party*, Edward, the discouraged husband, gropes in the darkness of restricted freedom. Unable to love his wife and caught in his own self-condemnation, he describes his despair in these graphic words:

> There was a door
> And I could not open it. I could not touch
> the handle.
> Why could I not walk out of my prison?
> .   .   .   .
> It was only yesterday
> That damnation took place. And now I
> must live with it.
> Day by day, hour by hour, forever and ever.

But I ask you, was it only yesterday that damnation took place? How long does the door to freedom beckon us? What forces combine to erect the bars of enslavement? Every decision we make restricts the opportunity for every other decision and narrows the range of our choice.

For this reason the decision of our relationship to God is basic. This is the momentous decision which we must all make and for which we are all responsible. When by some mysterious grace God touches the intimate center of our lives, at that point we accept or refuse on the basis that henceforth we belong to him or we do not belong to him. It is this decision that precludes all other decisions and in which all other decisions are caught up and properly assessed.

Walt Whitman once said, "All music is what awakes from you when you are reminded by the instruments." Commitment to God and trust in him are what keeps us aware of and awakens us to responsibility in all the decisions that make up our total life.

So, the hour strikes for each of us. Man stands before God. This is his day—a day of visitation and testing, a moment of judgment and a moment of grace. The past and the future meet and the source of life and freedom is ours. To miss it is to deny ourselves that for which we must forever seek, that which we shall eternally need. To miss it is to condemn ourselves to the soul-shriveling confines of limited freedom.

Prayer: Eternal Father, at the fork of the road today I decide for thee. Make me a captive to thy will that I may be free indeed. Amen.

Can We Begin Life Over Again?

> "Although you were dead because of your sins, . . . he has made you alive with Christ. For he has forgiven us of all our sins . . . and in him you have been brought to completion."—Col. 2:13, 14, 10 NEB

Is there a person alive who has not, at one time or another, expressed the desire to start life over again? Be honest now. How many times have you looked back over your life and wished that you could live it again? More times than you can number haven't you?

None are free of these anxious sighs. We have cheaply used what has been given us. We have held in our hands high and holy opportunities only to carelessly use them and cast them aside onto the dung heap of squandered hope. In blind haste we have hurried through days that were pregnant with possibility, failing to "turn aside and see" what significant contribution we could make. Thus those days were darkened by our shoddy labors and our calloused indifference. We have cruelly trodden on the hopes and dreams of others, poured the acid of our contempt upon them, and irreparably damaged their budding souls. And sin of sins, we have handled the pearls of God's grace and love with dirty and clumsy fingers. We have stood on God's holy ground with desolately arid souls, unaware of his presence. In our brash arrogance and smug pride we have stuck out our chests of self-assertion and said "no" to God, ordering life on our own terms and living life in our own way.

How casual it all seemed when we were setting the patterns of our lives. Little did we realize how deep were the ruts we were carving and how entangled we would be in the barbed wire of compromise, moral cowardice, selfish security, vacillation, deceit, half truths, and pride. These ruts get deeper and deeper until we realize how difficult it is to get out. Paul Laurence Dunbar wrote about it:

> This is the debt I pay
> Just for one riotous day—

Years of regret and grief,
Sorrow without relief.

Pay it I will to the end—
Until the grave, my friend,
Gives me a true release,
Gives me the clasp of peace.

Slight was the thing I bought,
Small was the debt, I thought,
Poor was the loan at best—
God! but the interest!

So, looking back over life, and seeing what we have carelessly done with it, we long for a chance to redeem it. We gaze wistfully over the horizon of time and experience, searching for some "land of beginning again."

But this is impossible. In fact, this is not our need. What we need is a *new* life, free of the shackles of the past that bind us, free of the gibbering ghosts of guilt, free of the stultifying sense of failure, free of the misery of self-condemnation, free to begin a *new* life, unhindered and unhampered by the crushing weight of past sin.

Amazingly, this is what the Christian faith offers. In talking about this promise Paul said, "Although you were dead because of your sins, . . . he has made you alive with Christ. For he has forgiven us all our sins . . . and in him you have been brought to completion." When we open our lives to Christ, responding to his offer, submissive to his will, we receive his gift of forgiveness and new life. He works his new creation within us! Mysterious? Yes, as mysterious as God bringing forth a bud from a bulb, a plant from a seed, fruit from a blossom. But it happens. Unlike the bulb and the seed and the blossom, which have no choice in the matter, it happens when we may say *yes* to Christ.

Prayer: We want to say *yes*, O Christ, but we have been going this way so long, it's difficult. Help us utter aloud now, with positive affirmation, that which struggles to be said in the depths of our souls: Yes. Amen.

No Longer in the Cellar

> "If you knew what God can give," Jesus replied, "and if you knew who it is that said to you, 'Give me a drink,' I think you would have asked him, and he would have given you living water!"—John 4:10 Phillips

William Barclay has told that in the Edinburgh congregation to which the great preacher George Matheson came, there was an old woman who lived in a cellar in filthy conditions. Matheson had been there some months preaching the magnetic gospel of Christ in his challenging way when Communion time came. In the Scotch Presbyterian tradition, an elder of the congregation called at the old woman's cellar with the card for her to sign in order to make Communion, but she was gone. Finally he tracked her down. He found her in an attic room. The woman's economic situation had not changed. There were no luxuries, but the attic was as light and airy and clean as the cellar had been dark and dismal and dirty.

23

"I see you have changed your house," the elder said to her.

"Ay," she answered, "I have. You canna hear George Matheson preach and live in a cellar."

I wish I could preach that way! That's what preaching ought to do for a person—move him from the cellars of life to the attics. That's what Jesus did. Wherever he went, people left their dark holes and clamored out into the sunshine of a new day. You could trace Jesus' footsteps through those Galilean hills by the changed lives that he left behind.

Here was Zacchaeus, settled down in his cellar of economic security, hated by the people from whom he collected taxes, and hazily knowing that something more significant than money existed somewhere. Then Jesus came. Short Zacchaeus stood ten feet tall in the sunshine of freedom from the chains of materialism after that luncheon with Jesus.

There was that Samaritan woman who came to the well at midday to escape the accusing stares and barbed words of her neighbors. She was living a sordid life in the musty basement of moral looseness and infidelity. She found Jesus at that well. He didn't rebuke her as she expected him to do. He expressed forgiveness and concern. In that moment she felt the fresh breeze of real love blowing in her life, and she knew that she could never live in that moldy basement again.

The list would be endless if we knew and could name those who have felt the same transforming power and have moved from the cellars of life to the attics because of Christ.

24

To test it, you have only to try. You can't live with Christ and seek to discover his spirit without finding the same thing happening to you. If you take him seriously, and allow him expression in your life, you'll move out of your cellar. Self-pity, prejudice, jealousy, pride, deceit, enmity, greed, bitterness, hatred—all the cold, damp, ugliness of basement living will be unsatisfactory to you. And in his love and forgiveness you'll find the power to ascend those steps to ground-level, and above-ground-level, living. Horatius Bonar knew it and prayed,

> In the still air the music lies unheard;
>   In the rough marble beauty hides unseen:
> To make the music and the beauty, needs
>   The master's touch, the sculptor's chisel keen.
>
> Great Master, touch us with Thy skilful hand;
>   Let not the music that is in us die!
> Great Sculptor, hew and polish us; nor let,
>   Hidden and lost, Thy form within us lie!
>
> Spare not the stroke! do with us as Thou wilt!
>   Let there be naught unfinished, broken, marred;
> Complete Thy purpose, that we may become
>   Thy perfect image, Thou our God and Lord!

This word may not move you out of your basement like George Matheson's preaching did the old woman. But Christ will—if you'll let him!

Prayer: We know now, O Christ, where the water of eternal life is. We have tasted it. Yet the pull of the basement is strong. Enable us to make the kind of commitment to thee that will move us up to attic living. Amen.

Facing Life Slightly Tight

> "Seek ye first the kingdom of God, and his
> righteousness; and all these things shall be
> added unto you."—Matt. 6:33 KJV

An Episcopal rector in New York City, John Ellis Large, has told of an experience at a cocktail party that shows something of the irresponsibility and despair of our day. It was evident that one of the guests had already fortified himself for the party by imbibing rather generously before leaving home. The gathering was small, therefore the good rector could not escape a confrontation with the man. After affable greetings and the disposal of the pleasant amenities, he looked at the rector with "eyes sadder than those of a beagle" and said, "The world is certainly in parlous state." Getting agreement, he went on with a solemn gaze and an earnest voice. Dramatizing his feeling, he emphasized his point by grasping the lapels of the rector's jacket, "I've spent a lot of time thinking about it, and I've come to an undeniable conclusion. This is it. In the face of the world's current crisis, a Christian gentleman has two choices. He can either confront the crisis *as* a Christian—or he can stay slightly tight all the time. . . . I have chosen the latter."

One doesn't know whether to laugh or cry at such a conclusion. No doubt it was not the result of some snap judgment. Perhaps he had come to this decision in a time of sobriety and seriousness. Having made up his mind, he would henceforth exercise his obligation to God and to his fellows through the haze of alcoholic dullness. As long as his liquor held out, so would he.

In dozens of different ways such as this we order our lives. We look at the condition of the world and conclude that things are so complex, and so impossible, that we can render little or no meaning to it. Our little drop of influence in the ocean of humanity will not be noted. Rather than facing the frustration of such seeming futility, we prefer to be indifferent. We accomplish this indifference by deliberate and artificial escapes from life as it is.

If this doesn't work, we content ourselves to move with the tides. Staying on the surface of things, we are easily swept here and there and we never have to buck the current.

In the crucial days of 1941 Winston Churchill commented, "Nothing is more dangerous . . . than to live in the temperamental atmosphere of a Gallup poll, always feeling one's pulse and taking one's temperature. . . . There is only one duty, only one safe course, and that is to try to be right and not to fear to do or say what you believe to be right." This is not always easy. It is certainly more demanding than the half-conscious approach that we can take by staying *slightly tight*. But the rewards of such responsible living are great enough to offset the frustration that we sometimes know. To have the certainty that we have acted boldly and have responded intelligently to the situations as they have arisen gives one a sense of direction and meaning that is more than adequate to overcome the futility that may seek to force itself upon us.

The soap-box preacher at the cocktail party may

be altogether right. We can face the crisis as a Christian, or we can stay slightly tight all the time. The choice is not simply between those specific alternatives, yet the choice is between the positions that the alternatives represent. We can live responsibly and thus meet our obligation to God and man. Or, we can live half-consciously, using different means to escape the demands that are made of us. The decision is ours.

Prayer: Our Father, the alternatives are ours. We can move with deliberate decision, or flounder indecisively. Give us the courage to face every issue *as* a Christian. Amen.

Life Dispersed on Ribbon Road

> "Commit thy way unto the Lord; trust also in him."—Ps. 37:5 KJV

My introduction to California was complete when I spent almost an entire weekend on the freeways. I know now what T. S. Eliot was talking about in one of his choruses from *The Rock:*

And now you live dispersed on ribbon roads,
And no man knows or cares who is his neighbour
Unless his neighbour makes too much disturbance,
But all dash to and fro in motor cars,
Familiar with the roads and settled nowhere.

Bumper to bumper, headlights glaring, nerves frayed, energy wasted, tempers flaring—there we were, all weekend—"dispersed on ribbon roads."

It came to me that perhaps this is the best symbol for modern man: *ribbon roads*. We spend most of our time in our cars. We know the roads, but we aren't settled anywhere. There is no deep feeling of belonging to the land or to an area as there was in a past day. This contributes to the insecurity that menaces our lives. Without roots we go with the wind like tumbleweeds. We are constantly on the move, but never really certain about the direction.

We are dispersed. The family unit has been shattered by our dispersion. Family members may live in Florida, California, Mississippi and Europe. The family ties that once contributed to solidarity are severed. Distances separate us and intimate communication is impossible.

We are scattered and there is no sense of community. My neighbors disperse each morning to go in several directions. One may be working in San Diego, another in Los Angeles. The feeling of community is hard to establish. Thus our lives are incomplete in lonely independence. The forces of modern living continually whirl us apart.

"And no man knows or cares who is his neighbor." Who are these people—the ones whose bumpers I touch, the ones whose bumpers touch me? This, too, is a symbol. The only intimacy we know is the cold contact of our chrome bumpers. For the most part we don't care who they are—unless they make too much disturbance, unless they don't move fast enough or fail to stay in their lane of traffic.

The outward condition is not going to change; rather it will get worse. A million acres of land in California will be dedicated to "ribbon roads" in the near future. The pattern is the same across the nation. Is there any hope for us? Is there some word to be said to these people living in a maze of asphalt?

A part of the answer is in the church. At her best the church is a faithful community of followers of Christ. Here, as nowhere else, man dispersed on ribbon roads can have a sense of belonging, a sense of security, a feeling of solidarity. Here, as nowhere else, he can know the meaning of neighborliness and can share in a creative program of fellowship and service. Above all, he can be encouraged and strengthened inwardly in order that he can withstand the pressures and problems of "life dispersed on ribbon roads."

Prayer: Dispersed as we are, our Father, we want to belong. Belonging to thee, may we find fellowship with others who sense this need. Amen.

DEDICATION

The Demands of Dedication

> "For you have been granted the privilege not only of believing in Christ but also of suffering for him."—Phil. 1:29 NEB

The demands of Christ are *total*. He makes no appeal for a halfhearted dedication. In fact, he accepts no offer of a less-than-complete dedication.

Our problem is at this point. Meister Eckhart wrote: "There are plenty to follow our Lord halfway, but not the other half. They will give up possessions, friends, and honors, but it touches them too closely to disown themselves." And yet this is necessary—a denial of self, complete obedience without any reservations.

The cause that comes closest to overshadowing Christianity in gaining adherents in this century is communism. The claims of this godless religion upon a disciple are total also. A minister in Montreat, North Carolina, gave Billy Graham a letter which eloquently portrays the dedication elicited. It was written by a young man to his fiancée, breaking off their engagement after he had become a convert to communism while vacationing in Mexico.

We communists have a high casualty rate. We're the ones who get shot and hung and lynched and tarred and feathered and jailed and slandered and ridiculed and fired from our jobs, and in every other way made as uncomfortable as possible. A certain percentage of us get killed or imprisoned. We live in virtual poverty. We turn back to the party every penny we make above what is absolutely necessary to keep us alive. We communists don't have time or money for many movies, or concerts, or T-bone steaks, or decent homes and new cars. We've been described as fanatics. We are fanatics. Our lives are dominated by one great overshadowing factor—the struggle for world communism. We communists have a philosophy of life which no amount of money could buy. We have a cause to fight for, a definite purpose in life. We subordinate our petty personal selves into a great movement of humanity, and if our personal lives seem hard, or our egos appear to suffer thru subordination to the Party, then we are adequately compensated by the thought that each of us in his small way is contributing to something new and true and better for mankind. There is one thing in which I am dead earnest and that is the communist cause. It is my life, my business, my religion, my hobby, my sweetheart, my wife and mistress, my bread and meat. I work at it in the daytime and dream of it at night. Its hold on me grows, not lessens, as time goes on. Therefore I cannot carry on a friendship, a love affair or even a conversation without relating to this force which both drives and guides my life. I evaluate people, books, ideas and actions according to how they affect the communist cause and by their attitude toward it. I've already been in jail because of my ideas, and if necessary, I'm ready to go before the firing squad.

A Christian considers such a testimony and examines his dedication. How earnest am I? How much of self have I reserved? What conditions am I placing on my commitment? How specific is my direction? How solid are my convictions? How willingly would I suffer? Would I suffer at all? Let these questions burn in your mind. Contemplate Paul's testimony as he considers our calling: "For you have been granted the privilege not only of believing in Christ but also of suffering for him."

Prayer: We have been halfhearted in our dedication, O Christ. We repent. Forgive us. Accept now the offering of our total selves—without reservations. Amen.

Merely Curious

> "Present your bodies a living sacrifice, holy, acceptable unto God, which is your reasonable service."—Rom. 12:1 KJV

In the second act of Chayefsky's play *Gideon,* the angel of the Lord recognizes that his chosen one has rejected him. Gideon has vacillated between love and disenchantment, between a desire to serve and a longing to be served. Finally, he turns away from the Lord's representative in a fit of resentment, and the angel, speaking for the Lord, says: *"I meant you to love me, but you are merely curious."*

Put this in personal perspective. What has been your relationship in Christian commitment? Has it been curiosity or love? Hold that question in your mind as you consider the general mood of religion today.

The past thirty-five years have witnessed a resurgence in religious interest. Membership rolls of church denominations and religious organizations have grown rapidly. More than 60 percent of our population in America belong to some religious body. If we drew a graph representing the mood of the past three or four decades, the line designating religious interest would rise sharply.

But—and this is the shocking fact—the line representing crime rate would rise even more sharply. There is a conflict here. When we have been most interested in religion, we have had a higher degree of criminal involvement on the part of the public. You answer the question. Have other influences affected the life of man more than the Christian church and other religious groups?

And the angel, speaking for the Lord, says: "I meant you to love me, but you are merely curious." Perhaps it is a true indictment. We have been merely curious.

The need of our day is vital commitment. Bonhoeffer, the martyr of Hitler's Germany, spoke realistically when he said, "When Christ calls a man he bids him come and die!" It was a realistic appraisal of discipleship because this is what happened to Bonhoeffer as a result of his commitment. He heard Christ's call; he came; he died!

Until those who are curious about the implications of Christianity can move from curiosity about the meaning of it all into a depth experience of love and devotion, we will not know the power of Christianity in our own lives and in the life of the world. Mere curiosity will not suffice to ease the suffering and misery of the world. It will not comfort the miserable who are in desperate need of God's love.

And the angel, speaking for the Lord, says: "I meant for you to love me, but you are merely curious." Is that word directed at you and me? Are we curious or consecrated?

Prayer: Loving Father, may our curiosity grow into consecration. Amen.

Your Religion: Escape or Involvement?

> "With thee is the fountain of life: in thy light shall we see light."—Ps. 36:9 KJV

One of the insistent needs of our lives is to escape from the intolerable clutches of reality. It is true that men of all ages have sought, and invariably found, what they thought was some reliable means of briefly loosing its steel grip.

Though it is a pulverizing indictment, still it is true, that one of the means used to escape reality is religion. We have developed in our day what one has called "escape-hatch religion." We like to have escape alleys in our avenues of altars. The author of the *Pen-ultimate* column in *The Christian Century* illustrated this so pungently in his reference to an architectural design for a

35

religious home. This home was designed with a private altar as one of the features of split-level living. The chapel was even shaped in the form of a cross (how religious can you get!). But, looking at the design's fine print, one found this note: "alternate studio, den, sewing room, etc."

Here was the escape clause. It took the zing and zest out of an otherwise admirable plan. The religious heart of the home was but an option. If you did not want the chapel, a place to pray, you could turn the space into a studio or den, you could have a place to sew or watch TV!

But not only do we want an escape clause in our religious commitment, often we use our commitment itself for escape. Many of us think that is what religion is—escape from reality. Worship for us functions as a retreat from a work-a-day world that is too much with us. For an hour on Sunday morning we can sing hymns, recite creeds, read scripture, hear the words of a sermon, and get away from whatever pressure is being brought upon us in our daily routine. People still think of us as in every way religious. America continues to be called a Christian nation when to a great degree all we have is a large group of tired people, writhing in the intolerable clutches of reality, seeking some relief from it on Sunday by going to their fashionable churches.

Ask yourself: "Is my religion escape or involvement?" Is my commitment a dedication to a great cause or a retreat from the perplexities and mysteries of life?

Religion at its highest can never be escape. It must be involvement. When the psalmist said, "The Eternal is my retreat," he was not suggesting any possibility of getting away from life. What the psalmist is talking about, and what religion at its highest does offer, is the strength to grapple with the difficulties and perplexities of life, to accept them, to become involved in them without being crushed by their power.

Prayer: May we discover, our Father, that life with thee is a practice of devotion that ends in involvement with the world. Amen.

From Death to Life

> "I am crucified with Christ: nevertheless I live; yet not I, but Christ liveth in me."
> —Gal. 2:20 KJV

Dietrich Bonhoeffer, to whom we referred in a previous meditation, was a leader of the Confessional Church in Germany at the time of Hitler's rise to power. He opposed this bloody movement of Hitler with all his strength and conviction and was imprisoned on April 5, 1943.

Even in prison and concentration camps, Bonhoeffer, by his indomitable courage, his unselfishness, and his goodness, greatly inspired all those who came in contact with him. He even inspired respect in his guards, some of whom became so much attached to him that they smuggled out of prison his papers and poems written there.

Leibholz, in his "Memoir" of Bonhoeffer tells,

On October 5, 1944, Bonhoeffer was transferred from Tegel to the main Gestapo prison in the Prinz Albrechtsstrasse in Berlin. Although fully aware of what he had to expect there, he was perfectly calm, saying goodbye to his friends as though nothing had happened. . . .

In February, [1945,] when the Gestapo prison in Berlin was destroyed by an air raid, [he] was taken to the concentration camp of Büchewald and from there to other places until he was executed by special order of Himmler at the concentration camp at Flossenbürg on April 9th, 1945, just a few days before it was liberated by the Allies.

Eberhard Bethge in his Foreword to Bonhoeffer's *Letters and Papers from Prison* tells:

[His] last weeks were spent with prisoners drawn from all over Europe. Among them was Payne Best, an English officer. In his book *The Venlo Incident* Best writes: "Bonhoeffer . . . was all humility and sweetness, he always seemed to me to diffuse an atmosphere of happiness, of joy in every smallest event in life. . . . He was one of the very few men that I have ever met to whom his God was real and close to him." And, again, "The following day, Sunday 8th April, 1945, Pastor Bonhoeffer held a little service and spoke to us in a manner which reached the hearts of all, finding just the right words to express the spirit of our inprisonment and the thoughts and resolutions which it had brought. He had hardly finished his last prayer when the door opened and two evil-looking men in civilian clothes came in and said: 'Prisoner Bonhoeffer, get ready to come with us.' Those words, 'come with us'—for all the prisoners they had come to mean one thing only—the scaffold.

"We bade him good-bye—he drew me aside—'This is the end,' he said. 'For me the beginning of life.' . . . Next day, at Flossenbürg, he was hanged."

This is the man who had said, "When Christ calls a man he calls him to come and die." He knew the meaning of discipleship. The day of martyrs has not passed.

I ask you, whose prisoner was Bonhoeffer? The

Gestapo? NO! He was a prisoner and slave of Jesus Christ. When did he die? When they hanged him in Flossenbürg that Monday morning in 1945? No, he died when he left the security of a status-quo life and realized the "cost of discipleship."

At the heart of the Christian faith is the fact that death precedes life. The death that really matters is not the enemy that ends our physical existence. What really matters is when we die to self and are born to Christ. This is the meaning of Christian discipleship. No wonder Paul cried, "It is no longer I who live, but Christ who lives in me" (RSV).

Prayer: Our Father, may we experience, before we die, the death that really counts—death to self that we might live to thee. Amen.

Something There Is That Doesn't Love a Wall

> "God was in Christ reconciling the world to himself, . . . and . . . has entrusted us with the message of reconciliation."—II Cor. 5:19

Something there is that doesn't love a wall,

. . . .

Before I built a wall I'd ask to know
What I was walling in or walling out,
And to whom I was like to give offense.
Something there is that doesn't love a wall,
That wants it down.

—from "Mending Wall"

I'm sure this is one of Robert Frost's most quoted poems because it deals with such an obvious factor in our existence: *walls*.

In actuality the poem is built around a contra-diction. While it maintains that "Something there is that doesn't love a wall," it also insists that "Good fences make good neighbors." Perhaps it is true that man cannot live without walls, boun-daries, limits, and, particularly, self-limitations. Yet, man resents walls and is happy when something

> sends the frozen-ground-swell under it,
> And spills the upper boulders in the sun.
> —from "Mending Wall"

Deep down, we don't like walls!

A few years ago I had the privilege of visiting Berlin. The ominous wall was a well-established fact at that time. The lives of both West and East Berliners were ordered around the fact of this confining barrier. Only a Berliner could capture the full impact of the wall. A visitor can only imagine what it must be like to live under such foreboding circumstances. It was dramatic enough for me, though. The ordeal of getting through the guards at Checkpoint Charlie, the stories of the daring efforts at escape, the toll of deaths resulting from those efforts, the drabness of the eastern sector when compared to the western, the fear and the sort of heaviness in the air that one senses when going from west to east, especially at night—all combine to give the tragic impact that the wall has on that divided city.

"Something there is that doesn't love a wall."

And yet, it is a symbol of our day. Walls are everywhere to be seen. The story of history is the story of erected walls—battered and broken by the storms of civilization, but restored; torn down on occasions to be erected in other places at other times. The story of man's relationship to man, whether as individuals or as nations, is the story of walls: walls of hostility, jealousy, hatred, prejudice. The story of man's relationship to God again is the story of a wall: the wall of estrangement, separation, alienation.

Can one miss the meaning of the metaphor in the Genesis story? Rebelling against God, Adam is driven "east of Eden." A cherubim and a flaming sword are placed between him and Eden. The "gardener" who had become a "rebel" is now a "fugitive." The wall between him and God had been erected by his disobedience.

Adam's story is the story of every man. In fact, Adam is every man. Rebelling against God, we become fugitives. Not only is our life thereafter a constant running away from God, it is a running away from self and from others. The walls are erected. Estrangement has taken place. We are separated from God, our fellowmen, ourself.

At this point Christ's coming into the world becomes relevant. The opposite of estrangement is reconciliation. Note the definition of the work of God in Christ. "God was in Christ reconciling the world unto himself, . . . and . . . has entrusted us with the message of reconciliation."

Return to my experience of the wall in Berlin. I never will forget a part of that experience which since has become a symbol for me of the total meaning of the Christian gospel and my own ministry. I forget whether I was in the western or eastern sector of that divided city, but the wall had been erected very near a church. In the church yard, at the brink of the wall, was a statue of Christ. It towered above the wall with outstretched arms as though reaching to the other side. The name of the church was the Church of Reconciliation.

This is the work of Christ, and this is the task to which we are called—the work of reconciliation. The walls that divide man and God, nation and nation, man and man, man and himself must be broken down. Only the love of Christ operating in our lives is sufficient for such a task.

Prayer: The walls are everywhere. They separate us from thee, from others, from ourselves. In the name of him who came to eradicate all walls, may we be instruments of reconciliation. Amen.

A Portion of Ourselves

> "The man who tries to save his life will lose it; it is the man who loses his life for my sake and the Gospel's who will save it."—Mark 8:35 Phillips

To establish direction in life we need to consider our present situation. We are writhing in the hell of self-preservation and self-centeredness and many of us can't understand why the fire is so hot. Rollo May, the eminent psychologist-author, in his book *Man's Search for Himself* observed, "Never before has a generation been so preoccupied with themselves, troubled with themselves, trying to find themselves." It's a sickness of self-centeredness of which we are victims. It's a poison that is spreading through the bloodstreams of our civilization, and the end can be but death. This is "I" trouble, not the member of our body with which we see, but the capital letter "I" that we use so often. It's what Wallace Hamilton calls "alphabetical heresy" —big "I" and little "u." It's the same battle that has always been the central problem of every man's life—how to get out of the center and put something else there.

I know many people today who are miserable. Almost every day I talk to someone whose life has dried up to nothing and whose existence is a monotonous humdrum of passing time. For the most part, they are living in the prison of self-interest. There is a parable in nature that teaches us here. A friend of mine called it to my attention. We were walking around our yard looking at the different plants, when we came upon a beautiful pelargonium. It was looking rather scraggly, though a few days before it had been filled with blossoms. Ted began to pull away all the wilted blooms. His contention was that the more of the blooms you took away, the more you would have. If you don't take the wilted ones away, they demand energy and food which the plant could expend on new and fresh flowers. Life is that way. *It adds up to zero when the only interest is self-interest.* It can expand to infinity when we realize that the only valid gift is a portion of ourselves.

We need this dedication in all of life. *We need it in marriage.* How many times do we seek to stay happy in our homes by giving gifts of a material nature. If our children aren't happy we buy more *things.* If our wives aren't happy we give them more gifts or remind them of how happy they should be because of what we are giving them already! What we need to give is a portion of ourselves.

In human relations this is the necessary ingredient. We don't buy a friend; friends can't be purchased. They come by the arduous process of self-giving. In race relations we should have learned by now that it is not enough to seek alleviation of laws and customs that have for so long oppressed the Negro. A chasm between the races has been dug by a steady stream of misunderstanding, prejudice, even hatred. This chasm will be bridged only through gifts of ourselves in personal relations.

I visited Watts in Los Angeles, shortly after the riots in August, 1965. The charred beams in burned-out buildings reminded me of the dark night of strife and hatred that we have known so long. The dry ashes blowing in the wind reminded me of the emptiness of so many of us in our understanding and appreciation of those who are different from us only in color.

We were driving along Central Avenue. On the corner of Central and Forty-third Place a huge building had been burned, and there on the front, facing Central, was an almost perfect cross. It was two huge beams that had been a part of the structure of the building, held together at the crossbeam with steel plates. They were charred black by the fire, and one end of the crossbeam was a mass of splinters where the beam had been broken as the structure collapsed. It was a jolting thing, standing about twenty feet high, dominant in the midst of the debris.

This was a revelation to me. I'm frustrated when I think in terms of what can be done for the "Watts" that exist around our nation. But I know

44

this: Whether we are talking about Watts, or illiteracy, or poverty, or loneliness, or homeless children—that charred cross suggests the answer. For the answer comes back to this word of Jesus, "The man who tries to save his life will lose it; it is the man who loses his life for my sake and the Gospel's who will save it."

The only valid gift we can offer is a portion of ourselves. In our sphere of activity and relationship, this must be the dedication we make.

Prayer: We know, our Father, though we seldom practice it, that we find our lives by losing them. Enable us to make the only valid gift a portion of ourselves. Amen.

A Measuring Rod for Christian Commitment

> "Oh, my dear children, I feel the pangs of childbirth all over again till Christ be formed within you."—Gal. 4:19 Phillips

Most of us need a measuring rod. We are practical-minded to the degree that we want this even in our spiritual lives. It is a dangerous thing, though, to seek this in the area of Christian commitment. We run the risk of setting ourselves up as judges of another's experience. This becomes a chief sin.

One's religious experience is an individual relationship to God, and that relationship cannot be violated by our judgment of it. However, as we look at the testimony of the New Testament and the early church, as we consider the lives of those we have known as committed Christians, we con-

45

clude that certain truths are going to characterize the lives of those who are totally committed to Christ. This, then, is our rod of measurement.

First, *a vital experience of God.* Religion is not something we defend by arguments; it is an experience that defends us. True Christianity is God-centeredness. It is, as Henry Scougal testified, "a union of the soul with God, a real participation of the divine nature, the very image of God drawn upon the soul, or, in the apostle's phrase, it is Christ formed within us."

The degree of this experience will depend upon the degree of our desire for it. In everything, everyday, we can practice God's presence. Brother Lawrence, the barefooted Carmelite, who cooked for the brothers in the monastery, so practiced the presence that he could say, "The time of business does not with me differ from the time of prayer; and in the noise and clutter of my kitchen, while several persons are at the same time calling for different things, I possess God in as great tranquility as if I were upon my knees at the blessed sacrament."

Brother Lawrence might have said with Edwin Markham,

> So here in the roar of mortal things,
> I have a place where my spirit sings,
> In the hollow of God's Palm.

Second, *inner purity.* Being a committed Christian involves a revolution of character. Experience of God purges us of bitterness, hatred, selfishness, pride, and other impurities. It replaces these with new life.

46

It sometimes appears that we are afraid of goodness. While science is continually fighting physical imperfections, we shy away from fighting spiritual and moral imperfections. We soon learn, though, that the closer we get to God the purer our motives become.

Third, *love of fellowman*. As we come to know and love God, we come to love his children, our brothers. A great saint once said, "Just as God bestows unmerited love on the Christian, the Christian in turn bestows love on every creature of God."

Fourth, *complete self-giving*. Where will Christian love lead us? How far will it compel us to go?

On a construction job a man saw that his son was going to be caught in a cave-in. Instantly he jumped into the hole, hovered over his son and took the full blow of the cave-in. When workers uncovered them they found the father dead from a blow on his head, but the son was living. The father's body had kept the dirt off him and enabled him to breathe until the workers saved him.

That is the kind of self-giving demanded of the committed Christian.

Reconsider them: a vital experience of God, inner purity, love of fellowman, and complete self-giving.

How is your commitment?

Prayer: We long to measure up, our Father. Yet we fail. Forgive our failure and set our feet on paths of renewed effort. Amen.

DETERMINATION

Holy Recklessness

> "No wonder we do not lose heart! Though
> our outward humanity is in decay, yet day by
> day we are inwardly renewed. Our troubles
> are slight and short-lived; and their outcome
> an eternal glory which outweighs them far.
> Meanwhile our eyes are fixed, not on the
> things that are seen, but on the things that
> are unseen: for what is seen passes away;
> what is unseen is eternal."—II Cor. 4:16-18
> NEB

In one of his books Paul Scherer tells of Sir
Francis Drake's sailors, who used to sit on the
rocky coasts of England telling the country lads
not about the pleasures of the sea but its dangers.
They talked of the raging winds and stout waves
and the gallant ships riding out the storms. These
were such captivating tales that the country boys

wanted it so much that they would run away from home in order to become a part of it.

When one contemplates the life of Christ and the call he makes, one realizes that the Christian life is something like that. It has that sort of appeal. Not many leaders captivate their would-be followers by demanding, "If any man would come after me, let him deny himself, take up his cross and follow." What boldness! What a way to get disciples; deny self, take up cross, follow me—this is a radical demand and it calls for abandonment.

The life to which we are called as Christians is one of *holy recklessness*. A lot of people I know have begun to ask seriously, "Where is all this going to take me? What does it really mean to get serious about the Christian life?" I can't answer those questions completely; I'm asking them myself. I can only say this: *the demands are for an utter abandonment to God and a submission to his will.*

When this sort of commitment is made, questions won't matter. We will be able to affirm with Paul, "No wonder we do not lose heart! Though our outward humanity is in decay, yet day by day we are inwardly renewed. Our troubles are slight and short-lived; and their outcome an eternal glory which outweighs them far. Meanwhile our eyes are fixed, not on the things that are seen, but on the things that are unseen: for what is seen passes away; what is unseen is eternal."

It takes eyes of faith to see this. Only a holy recklessness can achieve it, a sort of sanctified gambling. Turn again to Sir Francis Drake. He stood on the Isthmus of Panama and got his first glimpse of the Pacific Ocean. There it was in all its compelling mystery and challenge. Drake cried aloud, "Almighty God, of Thy goodness give me life and leave to sail once in an English Ship on that sea!"

When we look at the great sea of life to which God calls us as Christians, we know that we are beckoned to a holy recklessness and we pray, "O God, give us the spirit to respond." I'm excited at the possibilities. I get more excited every day! How about you?

Prayer: The sea of life is calling us. May we launch out with a holy recklessness, depending upon thee, O Christ, to captain our ship. Amen.

The Service of God in Our Lives

> "We are afflicted in every way, but not crushed; perplexed, but not driven to despair; persecuted, but not forsaken; struck down, but not destroyed."—II Cor. 4:8-9 RSV

One of the problems of our lives is that we want all the answers to all the questions at once. When we do not get these answers we despair. Rather than trusting God for one day at a time and living life at its fullest in the present moment, we look to the future, to tomorrow, next month, next year, even years from now.

This is the source of our neurotic dispositions. We are worrying about problems that haven't even arisen. And the chances are they will never arise. Yet, we try to face them today and find the answers now.

50

In light of this, what is the service of God to our lives? George Jackson, in a tribute to Robertson Nicol, who was for many years the editor of the *British Weekly,* unintentionally described this service in these words: "He flung down a bunch of keys for me, and has set me to opening doors for myself on every side of me."

This is what God does. He does not open all the doors. He flings down a bunch of keys and lets us find them and use them to unlock the doors for ourselves. In him we do not find a retreat from the pressures of life; we do not go into some monastery closing the door of daily living among men of the world behind us; but rather, life with him enables us to live with determination even amid the perplexities that once confounded us.

One thinks of Paul here. He was honest in his perplexity. "I do not understand my own actions," he confessed. "For I do not do what I want, but I do the very thing I hate" (Rom. 7:15 RSV). Aware of his inadequacies and failures, he became increasingly aware that the only answer was a constant contact with the source of life, God. He found that source in Jesus Christ. And yet he lived out his life as a Christian amid the stress and strain of a pagan world. His limitation in face of the perils he confronted only emphasized his frailty.

While living was always difficult, the reality of Christ in his life gave him determination and enabled him to say, "We are afflicted in every way, but not crushed; perplexed, but not driven to despair; persecuted, but not forsaken; struck down, but not destroyed."

Paul had found the true service of God in his life. His faith in God gave the confidence that no man can conjure up within himself. And so the same service of God is available for our lives. He casts a bunch of keys down before us. They are there waiting to be used to unlock any door of life through which we might enter.

Prayer: Thou hast given us the keys, O God; with determination may we busy ourselves fitting them to the right door. Amen.

God Is Involved in Our Personal Histories

"If the Lord had not been my help
my soul would soon have dwelt
in the land of silence."—Ps. 94:17 RSV

God knows our plights in the world and is involved in our personal histories. This is a bold affirmation and there are many people in our day who do not believe it. Like those in the days of the psalmist, they say, "The Lord does not see; the God of Jacob does not perceive" (Ps. 94:7 RSV). We believe that God may exist, but he is indifferent to our doings. If he is not indifferent, he is simply ignorant. With such a God we can do as we please, we think, without fear of consequence.

We have placed ourselves along side the drunken Rip Van Winkle, as played by Joseph Jefferson who, as he takes another drink, says: "I won't count this one." We are satisfied that if we do not count no one else will. And so we have drifted so far from center that we have lost reverence for the moral law.

This insensitivity leads to some obvious results. No longer is integrity the greatest virtue, but secrecy. The persons to be admired are not those with lofty character and high ideals, but those who have been successful in hiding their weaknesses. Such living may enable us to keep a good reputation, but our living will be trivial and unsatisfying. Listen to the psalmist as he answers such thoughts.

> He who planted the ear, does he not hear?
> He who formed the eye, does he not see? (Ps. 94:9 RSV.)

God knows our individual plights and is interested in our personal histories.

The implications of this truth are challenging and give us the determination to face life boldly. The first implication is that if God knows, then we cannot escape his judgment on our immorality and unrighteousness. At one of the wartime Lenten services in Washington's Church of the Epiphany, the Rt. Rev. Granville Gaylord Bennett had just begun to address the audience when his words were interrupted by the shrill blast of an air raid warning siren being tested atop the Capitol garage nearby. The Bishop paused. At the conclusion of the blast he pointed slowly upward and said, in not more than a whisper, "Had we listened to the 'still small voice of God,' we should not have this to listen to."

God's judgment is written into the fiber of the universe and we do not escape it.

A second implication of this foundation stone is a glorious one. If God knows, then God cares, so we do not suffer without his suffering with us. He shares our heartaches and sorrows. What meaning is given to life when we realize this. With what determination do we face the challenges around us!

The superintendent of a mission school read the text, "My yoke is easy." Turning to the children, she asked, "Who can tell me what a yoke is?" A little girl of ten said, "It is something they put on necks of animals." Then the teacher inquired, "And what is the meaning of God's yoke?" All were silent for a moment. Then the hand of a little four-year-old went up, and she said, "It's God's putting his arms around our necks!"

How we learn from children! God knows and cares. He is involved in our personal histories. His arms are around us. This often takes the form of a yoke, but when we know that it is God's yoke, we know that it is easy. This gives us the determination we need to face whatever comes.

Prayer: Put thy arms around us, our Father, that we might be sustained in all of life. Amen.

Suffering

> "Do you want to get well? . . . Get up, pick up your mat, and walk!"—John 5:6, 8 Goodspeed

Suffering belongs to life. Trouble in living is as certain as death. To try to remove this aspect of life is to seek to destroy a great part of its meaning. In the white heat of suffering, as the hammer blows of fate beat upon the anvil of life, we gain shape and form as human beings.

Suffering, then, is just as much a part of living as pleasure and the sooner we learn this the fuller our lives will be. Indeed, suffering may contribute far more to life than pleasure. Walt Whitman has spoken of this contribution of the resisting forces to life in these memorable lines:

Have you learned lessons only of those who admire you, and were tender with you, and stood aside for you? Have you not learn'd great lessons from those who reject you, and who brace themselves against you? . . . or dispute the passage with you?

Our only honest response is affirmative. The resisting forces of life have made significant contributions to us all.

In the Gospel of John there is an interesting story of Jesus' healing ministry that gives us a clue to our response to suffering. In Jerusalem, near the sheep market, was a pool called Bethesda. Five porticos surrounded the pool and in these a great number of sick people would lie. Blind, lame, withered, paralyzed, they would wait for the water to move. They believed that an angel would trouble the water and the first person who went into the water after it began to move would be healed.

At the Bethesda pool Jesus found a man who had been sick for thirty-eight years. What a strange question he asks the man: "Do you want to get well?" What sort of mockery is this? But Jesus knew. He sensed a part of the man's problem. It was his

55

attitude. Immediately the man began to bemoan the fact that nobody would help him. He had been there a long time, and, because others were not concerned about his illness, other sick people there at the pool always made it into the waters ahead of him.

Then Jesus speaks another strange word, "Get up, pick up your mat, and walk!"

Whatever you may think about the story, Jesus was making one thing clear. He put the stress on the man's attitude about himself. The invalid was so preoccupied with how others could help him that he had overlooked how he might help himself.

Here is our clue. The essence of wholeness or health is not dependent upon our freedom from suffering or trouble, but upon the attitude we take toward our suffering. Thus to be healthy does not mean that we are delivered from illness. In fact, wholeness may result from the redemption that comes to us in the midst of, and even because of, our suffering. Physical health emerges from an inner state of wholeness that comes when we have the right attitude toward our external situation and our symptoms of suffering.

When we see that suffering can be used creatively to discover the meaning of life, we are on the way to the kind of deliberate and determined living to which we are called.

Prayer: Our Father, help us sense the importance of our attitude toward our suffering. Give us the personal victory that comes when we are not victimized by symptoms of suffering. Amen.

Character Produces Hope

> "We ought to glory in our troubles, for we know that trouble produces endurance, and endurance, character, and character, hope, and hope will not disappoint us. For, through the holy Spirit that has been given us, God's love has flooded our hearts."—Rom. 5:3-5 Goodspeed

It is a strange word, isn't it? We ought to glory in our troubles. This is a new turn of things. We don't usually glory in our troubles. We moan and groan. We surrender to self-pity. We concentrate on our pitiful plight and so we wallow in the dust of our own weakness.

How different Paul's advice to the Roman Christians. This is one of his greatest lyrical passages and he almost sings the intimate joy of his confidence in God. Remember that Paul was writing to the Christians at Rome. It was not easy to be a Christian in Rome. Here Christians were burned at the stake to provide light for the sports of the emperor. Here they were fed to hungry beasts to entertain the lusty mobs. It was more than difficult to be a Christian at Rome. Paul knew this so he rose to this great height of Christian affirmation.

"We ought to glory in our troubles, for we know that trouble produces endurance, and endurance, character, and character, hope and hope will not disappoint us. For, through the holy Spirit that has been given us, God's love has flooded our hearts."

How differently do men face the same situation. One may be driven to despair, the other spurred to triumphant action. One may see the situation as the end of hope; to the other it may be seen as a challenge to greatness. Lord Reith once said, "I do not like crises but I do like the opportunities they provide."

We face situations differently according to the difference within us. If we have allowed ourselves to become weak and flabby by being beaten by circumstances, if we whine and grovel under affliction, when the challenge of the crisis comes we cannot do other than despair. On the other hand, if we insist on meeting life with head up, determined to face and conquer, we can meet each situation with hope for victory.

Paul now rises to his greatest height when he says that the character which has endured the test always emerges in hope, and the "Christian hope never proves an illusion for it is founded on the love of God."

Omar Khayyam in the *Rubaiyat* wrote wistfully of human hopes:

> The Worldly Hope men set their Hearts upon
> Turns Ashes—or it prospers; and anon,
> Like Snow upon the Desert's dusty Face,
> Lighting a little hour or two—is gone.

This is not the hope of the Christian. This is not what Paul was singing about. He has soaring confidence that the Christian hope will not disappoint us. We *know*, he said. He is not guessing, he is certain—certain because he is writing out of experience.

So here is a faith for us. Out of weakness we can be made strong. And the secret of it is this last sentence of Paul: "For, through the holy Spirit that has been given us, God's love has flooded our hearts." This is our faith, and this is our strength!

Prayer: With determination that is born in faith that cometh from thee, our Father, may we face life. Thus may we become conquerors, not conquered. Amen.

In Spite Of

> "And I am sure that he who began a good work in you will bring it to completion at the day of Jesus Christ."—Phil. 1:6 RSV

Omar Khayyam, the Persian poet who wrote wistfully of human hope, also looked upon the world with its misery and pain, and in fierce reaction to it proposed

> To grasp this sorry Scheme of Things entire,
> . . . shatter it to bits—and then
> Re-mould it nearer to the Heart's Desire!

How many of us share his feelings? We are ensnarled in adverse circumstances and long for some way to change things, to remold the world nearer our heart's desire.

We do not travel the Christian way long before we realize that this is a factor in life with which we have to deal: antagonistic circumstances are the rule, not the exception. To acknowledge this is the beginning point for developing the determination we need if we are to cope with these antagonisms.

Adversity is inevitable. We can rejoice in this, for the biographies of history confirm the fact that struggle and conflict are essential for growth and development.

With pain and suffering as present factors, we need, then, the determination to deal with them in such a way as to turn them into allies rather than enemies.

As a prisoner Paul wrote some of our most meaningful scripture. The Epistle to the Philippians is a thrilling example of this. Chained to a Roman guard, he wrote to his friends in Philippi, directing them to the fullness of life that is not dependent upon outward circumstance. In spite of his fetters he called them to this joy. How could he do it? What was the source of his determination?

"And I am sure that he who began a good work in you will bring it to completion at the day of Jesus Christ." There is the source. Paul was sure that once a person entered the Christian way with serious intention Christ would bring that commitment to completion. It was this confidence that gave him determination in spite of adversity.

Nail this down now: The Christian faith makes no claim about delivering us from difficult situations. Jesus himself was not delivered. It is precisely because he had no relief, no deliverance, no escape from the inevitable cross that we look to him for guidance. We feel that he was one of us, that he suffered as we suffer, that the antagonistic circumstances of life did not by-pass him. So, this strange man upon his cross keeps driving us back again and again to the struggles that are a part of the very fabric of life. It was Dame Julian of Norwich who expressed the truth so succinctly:

> He said not:
> Thou shalt not be tempested,
> Thou shalt not be travailed,
> Thou shalt not be afflicted;
> But He said:
> Thou shalt not be overcome.

Determination is ours when we know this. We shall not be overcome. Our commitment will be completed.

Prayer: It isn't easy, our Father, but you never said it would be. Give us the determination to continue *in spite of.* Amen.

Refuse to Be Defeated

> "Not as though I had already attained, . . . but I follow after, if that I may apprehend that for which also I am apprehended of Christ Jesus."—Phil. 3:12 KJV

When one looks at the giants of Christian history this aspect of their character looms large: *They refused to be defeated.* Paul personifies that trait. From imprisonment he wrote, "I don't feel as though I have attained, but I won't give up. I press on."

Spiritual growth depends on this—a refusal to

be defeated. This is the determination that drives us on.

A conquered Christian is a tragic sight. He is a refutation of all that Christ came to offer. Look at the early church. There were no organization, no buildings, no system of doctrine, no professional ministers, no New Testament, no prayer book or hymnal. There was only a group of men who had been captured by Christ and were, like Paul, pressing on to the mark of their high calling. They refused to be defeated because of that. Their calling had come from him. Submitting themselves to their calling, they were transformed— body, mind, and spirit. This transformation gave them indefeatable energy and indomitable courage.

What is the source of this spirit continuing in our lives today? Here it is: a tenacious commitment to Christ and the promise of his kingdom. When we make this commitment we can be constant in our discipleship and persistent in our witness, even though the rule of Christ is not obvious in the world, and even though vast numbers of people have not yet come to this commitment.

Man's determination and his amazing quality to "bounce back" is illustrated in recent history. Roy L. Smith in *The Future Is Upon Us* reminds us that

with the close of World War II tens of millions of Europeans lacked adequate food and many more millions were unemployed. More than half the great cities of the continent lay in ruins; somewhat in excess of 30,000,000 were listed as displaced persons. Hope had fled; transport was at a standstill; black markets were the common markets; morals were in eclipse; currencies were utterly unreliable; and rubble filled the streets of villages, towns, and cities. Hundreds of settlements had been completely destroyed; industrial installations were demolished; and hundreds of thousands—perhaps even millions—of human bodies lay buried under the debris. In spite of all this gloom and horror, however, there has been an amazing recovery. "Europe this side of the Soviet bloc is the most prosperous area of its size and population on the earth."

If this quality is a part of mankind in general, how much more dominant it should be in Christian man. We've been called by Christ. The promise of his kingdom is ever before us. We must refuse to be defeated!

Prayer: Sensitize us, O Christ, to our calling. Enable us to press on to this mark, determined by thy grace to overcome. Amen.

DISCIPLINE

The Kingdom Door Is Narrow

> "Strive to enter by the narrow door; for many, I tell you, will seek to enter and will not be able."—Luke 13:24 RSV

George A. Buttrick in his discussion of this text in *The Interpreter's Bible* says: "The kingdom door is narrow." Jesus used this figure in response to the question, "Lord, will those who are saved be few?" The "sharpness of Jesus' answer seems to show that the questioner was self-righteous. People then as now debated the number of the elect. Now, as then, . . . the debaters took it for granted that they were surely among the chosen." Yet, Jesus speaks sternly: "Strive to enter by the narrow door; for many, I tell you, will seek to enter and will not be able."

Dr. Buttrick continues: "Men may peer into God's future," as Jesus is saying, "but they cannot see." Though the kingdom may stretch out into ever-expanding fields of experience, though the vistas be wide and the horizons unlimited, still the "entrance gate is narrow; man may not enter except by the struggle of self-denial."

One may respond that the Christian is being bigoted when he makes such a proclamation as this. One may think that Jesus is trying to squeeze everyone into the mold of the same experience. It isn't so. This is the solid conviction that to enter the kingdom one must willingly give himself in devotion and discipline for "narrow is the gate that leads to life and few there are who will enter."

You may retort, why that's selfishness. Ah, no! Selfishness with "its moneybags and full-length mirrors is precisely the baggage that a man must cast away if he would enter that narrow gate."

Again, you may say that there is cruelty in the requirement. We turn again to Dr. Buttrick:

There is no cruelty in the requirement; mystery, indeed, but not cruelty. A scholar must "scorn delights, and live laborious days"; an athlete must eschew rich food, and subject himself to discipline; an artist must give weary hours and days to practice; a saint must pray and pray, and then deny himself so as to live as he prays. For Jesus the gate was as narrow as a cross. But there is no cruelty: faith in Christ is neither an epicureanism that would make life promiscuous [eat, drink and be merry], nor an asceticism that would leave life mutilated; it is rather a discipline that leads life to heaven, as the pruning of a plant gives a lovelier bloom.

This is what Jesus is talking about. The kingdom has a narrow door. To enter that door demands discipline and devotion. It demands self-sacrifice and self-denial.

Prayer: We are so flabby in our living, O Christ. We contemplate thy devotion and discipline and cry, "Woe is me." Forgive our "ease in Zion." We determine, with thy help, to enter the narrow door. Amen.

Adversity Often Brings Life

> "For I have learned to be content, whatever the circumstances may be. I know now how to live when things are difficult and I know how to live when things are prosperous. In general and in particular I have learned the secret of facing either poverty or plenty. I am ready for anything through the strength of the one who lives within me."—Phil. 4:11-13 Phillips

In the western part of our country there is a lodgepole pine tree that anticipates adversity and turns it into life. The foresters in that section have discovered that this tree sheds a very hard seedpod, which may remain in the ground unbroken for twenty, thirty, or forty years. Then the day comes when a forest fire sweeps over the home of this tree in the Rocky Mountain area. All life is destroyed. But no! The fire also cracks the hard pod, and thus releases the seed. Within a few years new life and a new forest are begun.

Here is a challenge to man. Most of us know adversity. There are many of us in the midst of trouble even now. This is almost as common as eating and breathing.

How different are our reactions to trouble and adversity. Some of us try to run away from it, or we refuse to believe the fact of it. Others hit against another person blaming that person for what has happened. Still others blame God and become recluses.

We ought to remember that our trouble is not unique. Nor is it an act of God. It is a part of our experience, and it brings us to the place where we share what others have already experienced—the pain of loneliness, the hurt of sorrow, the oppression of adversity.

It does us no good to become resentful and bitter. Rather, let us accept the adversity and see in it an opportunity for life and growth.

Another fact of nature can be a challenge to us here. Look at the oyster. One day into its shell comes a tiny grain of sand. The grain of sand is an intruder, an alien thing, really a catastrophe that imposes pain and distress. What can the oyster do? Someone has suggested four responses. Metaphorically speaking, the oyster can shake its fist in the face of God and openly rebel. Or, it can say, "It can't be true!" Or, it can exemplify great fortitude, courage, and determination. It can say, "This thing has happened to me. It is painful, but it cannot be helped. Since I must endure it, I'll bear it like a man." This is commendable. But there is still another thing the oyster can do. It can recognize the grim intruder and turn it into something beneficial, in fact, something very valuable. The oyster can build upon that grain of sand, slowly, patiently, and with infinite care, covering it with a layer of plastic, milky-like substance and gradually make a pearl. What is the pearl? It is a thing of pain and trouble that has been transformed—made into a thing of wondrous beauty and delight.

Here is a lesson we ought to learn. We can turn *our* adversity into life, our pain into joy, our sorrows into delight. And, if we can't go this far, at least we can find in our adversities an opportunity to understand and to serve others whose adversity may be far greater than ours. Perhaps the seedpod of life will be cracked in the fires of our experience. Maybe we can make pearls out of painful grains of sand.

Prayer: Eternal Christ, teach us how to live when things are difficult. May we find thy secret of turning a cruel cross into an instrument of salvation and life. Amen.

Waiting

"I will wait for the Lord . . . and I will hope in him."—Isa. 8:17 RSV

Patience! It is the virtue most lacking in most of our lives. Rudyard Kipling makes this a requirement of possessing the world and being a man: "If you can wait and not be tired of waiting."

This is one of the hardest lessons to learn. It is difficult to realize that we serve best sometimes by simply waiting. This requires ardent discipline.

There is an interesting episode in the life of the great prophet Isaiah. In the early chapters of the book of Isaiah, the prophet's autobiographical memoirs are recorded. In the eighth chapter there is the record of this prophet withdrawing from the active prophetic ministry. G. G. D. Kilpatrick in *The Interpreter's Bible* says, "He has spoken for God, and the message has been finally rejected by king and people alike. He then declares his purpose to become a spectator of the debacle which must ensue." "Bind up the testimony, seal the teaching among my disciples. I will wait for the Lord, who is hiding his face from the house of Jacob, and I will hope in him." (Isa. 8:16-17 RSV.)

There comes a time in the life of all of us when there is nothing to do but wait. We have done our work. We have made our witness. We have spoken our word. And now we must let God work in the situation however he will.

How hard it is! How hard it is for a minister. He preaches as God inspires him to preach. He sows the seed of God's word. It is so slow to take root. In fact, it seems more often than not that it will not germinate at all. The minister must remember that as Kilpatrick says, "in God's strategy there is a place for silence and the pause is one of his devices."

How hard it is for family members and friends of alcoholics. This is one of the thorniest problems in dealing with the alcoholic. As much as we want to help, as deeply as we love, as concerned as we are, still we have to wait. We have to wait until the alcoholic himself realizes his own need and is ready for our ministry.

How hard it is for parents. While we may maintain strict discipline, we should never be dictators. And there comes a time when we have to allow such freedom that our children may not do as we would like. Yet, we have to allow choice so maturity will come. So we have to wait.

It may help us to remember during these times of lonely waiting that God has to wait, too. Kilpatrick puts it thus: His "purpose of redemption is constantly thwarted by the indifference of men. He cannot compel obedience without invading the freedom he has given them. The irresistible and indisputable are weapons God cannot use to save us. Therefore he must needs let us go our own stubborn and foolish ways until life brings us up short, and we, beaten to our knees and realizing our own misery and helplessness, are at last ready to hear his word. God at times seems to withdraw from the human scene in order that we may learn our need of him."

How well Kipling knew: "If you can wait and not be tired of waiting." We need to learn that.

Prayer: We wait on thee, our Father. Enable us to wait *patiently.* Amen.

Discipline the Mind

> "The kingdom of God is within you."—Luke 17:21 KJV

> The mind is its own place, and in itself
> Can make a heaven of hell, a hell of heaven.

John Milton knew what he was talking about, as we see in these lines from *Paradise Lost.* He knew the self-made hells of which we are all victims. From another perspective, but saying the same thing, Omar Khayyam wrote in the *Rubaiyat,* "I myself am heav'n and hell." It is true, isn't it? Our minds are the final arbiters of peace or conflict, of joy or sorrow, of hope or despair.

This is what Jesus was giving positive expression to when he said, "The kingdom of God is within you." Heaven is there—or hell is there!

If this is true, it is terrifyingly true. The demand for a disciplined mind may well be the greatest demand to which we can respond. Anne Morrow Lindbergh spoke to this great need when she said: "The problem is . . . how to remain whole in the midst of the distractions of life: . . . The solution for me, surely, is neither in total renunciation of the world, nor in total acceptance of it. I must find a balance somewhere." Then she goes on to say that the balance is found when we learn the "art of shedding."

This "art of shedding" is a part of the mind-discipline we must practice if we would be whole. How many memories have we stored up within our mind-attics that ought to be pitched. These memories make for some rather scorching hells. Just at the time when we don't need any added anxieties, some stored-away-memory that brings burning guilt sticks out its head and begins to mock us. These should have been evicted from our minds long ago. The richness of life is constantly threatened by these memories.

Not only must we discipline ourselves in the "art of shedding," we must also practice the art of *selective intake*. We clutter up our minds with so much trash. Our reading and attention habits are so sloven. Since our mind is the seat of heaven or hell we need to be more careful about what we take into it.

Harry Stack Sullivan talks about the security operations of people. He says one tends to be "selectively inattentive" to anything which threatens his sense of security. This is a bad practice when it becomes the habitual pattern of behavior for a person. It prohibits all opportunities to try anything else and thus a change in behavior becomes increasingly difficult. There is a sense, though, in which this is a good practice. We need to be *selectively inattentive* to the poison that would corrupt and corrode our minds.

If we fed our bodies on the same kind of toxic food that we feed our minds, we wouldn't last very long. Yet we keep stuffing our brains with it. Little wonder that we are torn with conflict. We have let loose all sorts of antagonistic forces in our minds and they are at war.

We need to be selectively inattentive if we would escape this conflict.

Finally, every idea that knocks on the door of our mind doesn't deserve a permanent abode. We don't have to be rude and not answer the door. It's all right to entertain the different ideas. But we don't have room for all of them to stay. The sooner we recognize this and bid them good-bye the better off we are.

Have you found the meaning of Jesus' word, "The kingdom of God is within you"? Heaven is there—or hell is there. Whether hell or heaven depends on how we discipline our minds.

Prayer: We are trying, Father, but so much clamors for our attention. We have not learned to be single-minded, but we are working on it. Help us to drive on. Amen.

Overcoming Loneliness

> "Turn to me and have pity,
>   for I am lonely and low."—Ps. 25:16 Moffatt

An enterprising bar operator in Los Angeles sensed the predicament of man and sought to capitalize upon it. A large marquee over the door of his business signaled passers-by: *Lost a Friend—Find Another One Here!*

Man longs to love and be loved. He longs to relate to others in a warm intimate fashion. Our iron-cold culture does not always allow this. So one of our big feelings is that of being "cut off," lonely. The psalmist in the long ago experienced this and cried to God, "Turn to me and have pity, for I am lonely and low."

Mary Chase's play *Harvey* confronts us dramatically with the result of this lack of fellowship for which we crave. There is a significant degree of tenderness, serenity, and sparkle in her main character, Elwood P. Dowd. He had genuine affection and interest in people. Yet, the tragedy of the drama is that Elwood can retain the truly human sensitivities only when he is firmly braced against the world's reality by a continual flow of alcohol. He finds personal tenderness and friendliness in the bar. He finds it with a companion of his fantasy, Harvey. So he explains to the psychiatrist why his regular visitation to the bars was so important.

Harvey and I sit in the bars and we have a drink or two and play the juke-box. Soon the faces of the other people turn toward mine and smile. They are saying: We don't know your name, mister, but you're a lonely fellow.

73

Harvey and I warm ourselves in all those golden moments. We have entered as strangers, soon we have friends. They come over. They sit down with us. They talk with us. They tell us about the big, terrible things they have done . . . the big wonderful things they will do . . . their hopes, their regrets, their loves, their hates. All very large, because nobody ever brings anything small into a bar. Then I introduce them to Harvey. And he is bigger and grander than anything they offer me.

Deliverance from loneliness came for Elwood only in the fantasy born not of reality but of the hypodermic of alcohol. We must find another deliverance.

To be alone is the greatness and the burden of man. It is no small job to whip the demon of loneliness. It requires more than human resources, for this is a Philistine giant that would slay us. That we are attacked by it is a certainty. How, then, can we brace ourselves against it? How can we discipline ourselves to overcome it?

First, we must learn to love. This sounds trite, but it is really profound. I have never known a chronically lonely person who really loved. Nor have I known a person who really loved who was often lonely. When in deliberate, outgoing good will to others we involve ourselves in intimate relationships, the possibility of loneliness diminishes almost to zero.

Second, we must accept the fact that sometimes our love will be rejected. No matter how great our efforts there will come the time when those we seek to love will reject our overtures. The sting of loneliness at such a time will be almost unbearable. Our sustaining strength comes in the knowledge that our responsibility is to love—not chart response.

Finally, we must know the source of real fellowship. Depth relationships that are the permanent cure for loneliness are not rooted in human soil alone. There must be a divine additive. God becomes a part of the fellowship, and so our relationships are in Buber's fine designation "thou-thou" relationships. In such depth of feeling and appreciation loneliness is ministered unto, and we become ministers to those who are lonely.

Prayer: Turn to me and have pity, for I am lonely and low, O God. Having experienced thy visitation, may I be enabled to lift others out of the pit of loneliness. Amen.

Finding Solitude and Using It

> "And when he had sent the multitudes away, he went up into a mountain apart to pray: and when evening was come, he was there alone."—Matt. 14:23 KJV

In the previous meditation we talked about overcoming loneliness. There is a difference between loneliness and solitude. Paul Tillich has reminded us that our language has wisely sensed two sides of man's being alone. It has created the word "loneliness" to express the pain of being alone, and the word "solitude" to express the glory of being alone.

Learning to use solitude is one of the primary ways of overcoming loneliness. In fact, loneliness can ultimately be conquered only by those who can bear solitude and turn it into creative use.

Solitude is the glory of being alone. But it is not easy to find. This is our first problem. Our day is one of masses and crowds. To find the time and the place to be alone is a difficult task.

Alfred North Whitehead said, "Religion is what man does with his solitariness." Though not altogether true, this is true to a marked degree. It is true enough to cause us to realize that we cannot develop the deep wells of response to divine intimations unless there is found some time for solitude. Against the hectic busyness of our too-crowded and too-rushed days we must discipline ourselves to find time to be alone. It may mean an earlier rising, or a later retiring. It may mean giving up some social involvements. Whatever it means we cannot develop spiritually as we should without it.

Here is the bigger problem. How do we use it when we find it? First we need to eradicate the thought that we ought always to be *doing* something. Some power from hell has wormed its way into our mind and has convinced us that if we aren't always doing something we aren't accomplishing anything. Nothing could be further from the truth.

We need to learn to "do nothing" in our solitude. When we master this we can begin to meet ourselves. I remember a day on the beach that had been planned for quiet study. Somehow, in getting away with all the paraphernalia, lunch, and suntan lotion, the books I had planned to read were left behind. But it was one of the most meaningful days I have spent. In those hours of solitude I became acquainted with myself again. Some of the things I discovered about myself were pleasing, but many things were disturbing. It is only through such an acquaintance with myself that I can change and grow, can commit and feel.

We can't, however, reserve our time of solitude for the day when we might be caught somewhere without something to do. We must deliberately seek it, and finding it, endeavor to stay acquainted with ourselves.

Not only are we to meet ourselves in solitude, we're to meet God there. Jesus felt the necessity of this. "And when he had sent the multitudes away, he went up into a mountain apart to pray: and when evening was come, he was there alone." One can't help wondering what went on between Jesus and God on those occasions when he sought this kind of solitude.

According to the Scriptures, Jesus spent little time in formal prayer. I have an idea that in moments such as this he did very little talking. Very little word forming and conversation took place. It was, no doubt, a time of deep silence as Jesus sought to bring his spirit into communion with God. However he did it, we know that his innermost self was elevated to God and was immersed in God's spirit.

Solitude becomes, then, a difficult thing. To use it meaningfully requires discipline. Here we find ourselves and we find God. If we can bear it, we will face ourselves and the Eternal as his presence shines through the face of Christ.

Prayer: Make us earnest in our efforts to find solitude, our Father. In that solitude may we experience being alone, but not lonely—for there may we find thee. Amen.

Selling Better Living Cheaper

> "If any man will come after me, let him deny
> himself, and take up his cross, and follow me."
> —Matt. 16:24 KJV

One of the great corporations of the South has a very striking motto. It has come to mean more through the forty years since its adoption. The motto is "Selling Better Living Cheaper." That's an attractive slogan, isn't it? We are all interested in better living, aren't we? Especially are we interested in it if we can get it cheaper. It appears to be first-rate thinking on the part of this company: "Selling Better Living Cheaper." This is what the multitudes are interested in, the best—but cheap.

The climate of our day is well expressed in the episode of a woman who went into a store to buy a game of chess. "Tell me how to play it as you wrap the package," she said to the salesman. We are not too unlike that. We want the best, but we want it without paying for it. We are interested in getting something for nothing. Gone, to a great degree, is the day when man knew that if anything worthwhile came to him, it came as a result of hard labor and sacrifice. I wonder what would happen if someone advertised, *We sell the best things in life but they will cost you— they will cost you dearly*. The multitudes would not flock to the sales counters as they do on bargain days. The advertiser would not make a lot of money. Yet it would be interesting and refreshing to see what would happen.

In essence this is what Christ says: *Here are the best things in life, but they will cost you.* James

78

Stewart tells of how Napoleon, when an artillery officer at the siege of Toulon, built a battery in such an exposed position that he was told he would never find men to man it. But he had a surer instinct. He set by the side of it a placard: "The Battery of Men Without Fear." And it was always manned.

Something instinctive within man calls him to such a challenge. For this reason the Peace Corps has met with amazing response. This is the reason Christ is so impelling. While all around others are offering a crown, he offers a cross. While others are saying, "eat, drink and be merry," he says, "deny thyself." While others offer a primrose path of dalliance, he says, "the gate is narrow and the way is hard that leads to life." *Here are the best things in life, but they will cost you!*

Robert J. McCracken recalls a story that illustrates this spirit of being willing to pay for what is right and good and worthwhile. In 1830 Benjamin Constant, the French philosopher, received a message at the hands of his friends in Paris who were overthrowing the Bourbons. "A terrible game is being played here: our heads are in danger: come and add yours."

A thrilling challenge, I would think. But are we able to meet it? The best things in life are yours—*but they cost you*. Will you pay?

Prayer: Eternal Christ, open our eyes to the fact that the best things in life *cost*. Thou who didst pay the ultimate price, enable us to pay the price of following thee. Amen.

DEVOTION

More Than We Are

> "Here and now we are God's children. We
> don't know what we shall become in the
> future. We only know that, if reality were to
> break through, we should reflect his likeness,
> for we should see him as he really is!"—I John
> 3:2 Phillips

On the first page we find where Margueritte Harmon Bro gets the mind gripping title of her marvelous book *More Than We Are*. Here it is:

In Cabeza de Vaca's account of his journey from Florida to the Pacific, between the years 1528 and 1536, he tells how the Indians came to him and his companion asking them to cure the sick. The two white men were themselves half starved, lost and filled with blank despair but the Indians felt that being white men they had superhuman power and could use it if they wanted to. Cabeza de Vaca felt that they had no such power. "But we had to heal them or die," he wrote. "So we prayed for strength. We prayed on bended knees and in agony of hunger." Then they blessed each ailing Indian—and saw that the sick were being healed! Truly it was to our amazement that the ailing said they were well. Being Europeans, we thought we had given away to doctors and priests our ability to heal. But here it was, still in our possession."

Now listen to de Vaca as he goes on: "It was ours after all; we were more than we thought we were— To be more than I thought I was—a sensation utterly new to me."

So there's the revelation: "We were more than we thought we were." Isn't that a gripping idea? *More than we are!*

Most of us want to be more than we are, don't we? It's true throughout life. Little children dream of the day when they will be youth; youth of the time when they will mature to adulthood; and adults continue to burn with desires, hidden and expressed ambitions. Cradle to crematory, it's the same story: we want to be more than we are.

We were in the mountains recently. It was another world for our children. Kim, our six-year-old, asked me why I didn't move to the mountains and build houses and cut wood rather than be a preacher. And at times, I must confess, I feel such would be a good idea. We want to be more than we are. We have our ambitions, our goals, our desires in life. They are more than we are, yet, when we realize them, the longing is still there: we want to be more than we are.

I'm glad we're this way. It adds so much spice to life. That man who is dead to desire, dull to new ideas, blunt in his perception, insensitive to mystery—that man is not very much alive.

81

God has set eternity in our hearts. We want to be more than we are! Man is the only animal whose desires increase as they are fed. This is the way it is. No matter what we have we are never fully satisfied. We have been brought under the spell of a gnawing discontent.

How is it possible, you ask? There are a lot of ways to become "more than we are." By the use of a sanctified imagination, by the commitments we make, through prayer and worship, through fellowship—all these enable us to become more than we are. But here is the foundation of it all: "Here and now we *are* God's children. We don't know what we shall become in the future. We only know that, if reality were to break through, we should reflect his likeness, for we should see him as he really is!"

You want to be more than you are? Accept your sonship to God. Through a life of prayer discover his power to live as a true son should.

Prayer: We can be more than we are, O Christ, if only we will accept thy will for us. Enable us to do so. Amen.

How Earnest Is Your Prayer?

"Lord, teach us to pray."—Luke 11:1 KJV

"O Lord, save us from a brief prayer and a long coffee break."

That's a timely prayer, for the pattern of our day is a "brief prayer and a long coffee break."

We have too much passing for prayer today that

is only glib habit. We don't really pray; we say prayers.

How earnest is your prayer? With what seriousness do we take this discipline of spiritual devotion and meditation? How slovenly do we approach the act of prayer! How haphazardly do we enter into this most holy time of our life!

Ladies, you know this experience. A weary day has passed. Everything has gone wrong. The children have grated on your nerves. The neighbors have been especially "tedious and tasteless." The husband was late for dinner, and the food was cold. Finally, the children are off to bed; you do the dishes and then remember a club meeting the next morning for which you have made no preparation. You work on that for an hour. It's 11:30 now; you've been up since 6:30 in the morning, and you get into bed with the weariness of seventeen hours upon you. Then you try to pray. You say two or three sentences of "God bless this and God bless that," and you are asleep.

Men, you know the experience. The office has been hectic. The other workers have rubbed you in every sensitive spot. You failed to make the sale that you had been cultivating and counting on for four months. The boss was especially irritable. The customers were all complaining about the service they were getting. The client couldn't understand why you didn't have his work finished. The Community Chest was dogging you to get your calls made. You come home. The wife has been involved in a row the children had in the neighborhood and supper isn't ready. You have barely eaten when you have to go to some meeting. Home again at ten. You relax a minute watching

TV. The minute turns into an hour. By now your wife is asleep. You tumble into bed and mumble a few words that you call prayer, and begin another night of tossing and turning.

And we consider this prayer! Then, when some tragedy arises in our individual lives or in our homes, we try to pray. The words we seek to say turn to dust on our lips. There is no communication with God. Our hearts are barren.

What is the problem? We can't have God when we want him, at our own whim. We must have him on his terms, not ours. His terms involve not a spasmodic effort at communication now and then, but constant communion. It involves surrender of our wills to him. It involves disciplined devotion. If he comes into our lives, it is not to help us with our little aims, but to make our aims bigger; to transform us into his likeness and to enlarge our goals to his size.

In that light how earnest is your prayer? Is there any real sincerity in it? Any discipline? Is there any willingness to allow Christ to really live in you? Is there any surrender?

Prayer: Lord, make us earnest in our praying. Amen.

Kindle the Flame

> "God is light and in him is no darkness at all."—I John 1:5 KJV

Oliver Wendell Holmes spoke of people who "die with all their music in them." The tragedy of too many of us is here: we have never cultivated the music of devotion within. A tiny flame is there, but we never kindle it. Deep within us all the faint fire burns low, waiting to be fanned until it bursts into a blazing fire.

God is light. In him there is no darkness. He has set eternity in our hearts. This eternity struggles for expression, continuously pressing upon the time limitations in which we have imprisoned it.

The full glow of this flame has been called the inner light, the light within, the divine center, infinite life, and numerous other names. Thomas Kelly says in his book *A Testament of Devotion,* "It is a Light Within which illumines the face of God and casts new shadows and new glories upon the face of men. It is a seed stirring to life if we do not choke it. It is the Shekinah of the soul, the Presence in the midst. Here is the Slumbering Christ, stirring to be awakened, to become the soul we clothe in earthly form and action. And He is within us all."

However we talk about it, the truth is that we have an untapped resource of power, an amazing capacity for communion with God which is limited only by our misunderstanding, or our unconcern, or our unwillingness to pay the price of kindling the flame.

Two presuppositions are necessary as we begin to kindle the flame. One, God *is;* two, fellowship with him is possible. Few, if any, reading this, would have any problem with the first supposition —God *is*. Many have difficulty with the second —fellowship with God is possible. We talk about prayer, but few of us really pray. Perhaps it isn't that we disbelieve; we simply haven't entered into the *fellowship*. Is not George Macdonald's confession ours? " 'O God,' I cried, and that was all. But what are the prayers of all the universe more than expansions of that one cry? It is not what God can give us, but God that we want."

This is the *beginning* of prayer. The great mystics of the ages would affirm that it is, too, the end of prayer. God is; fellowship with him is possible.

Will you believe it? Those who have believed and have tested it in practice, in roarous voice acclaim the joy that has been theirs. They have tapped an inexhaustible source of joy; they have found a fountain to which they can turn with a thirst that is never quenched; they have opened their lives and the wind of the Spirit has fanned the tiny flame until it is a raging fire. While they now laugh at their puny lives at beginning, they know that far stretches of growth are yet ahead.

Will you begin now? Kindle the flame!

Prayer: Loving God, we know that you *are*. We know, too, that fellowship with you is possible. We are ready now. Accept our efforts at beginning. Amen.

Beginning to Pray

> "O send out thy light and thy truth: let them lead me."—Ps. 43:3 KJV

And I said to the man who stood at the gate of the year: "Give me a light, that I may tread safely into the unknown"

And he replied:

"Go out into the darkness and put your hand into
the Hand of God.

That shall be to you better than light and safer than
a known way."

These simple lines of M. Louise Haskins from
"The Gate of the Year," with which we are all
acquainted, express our trepidation at beginning
to pray. And yet the certainty of God's presence
is ours as we launch the venture.

We learn to pray by praying. For some of us
the journey will be a swift run; for others, a
steady walk; and for others, a painful creeping.
But all will reach the goal! Let us take the first
step.

Center down! We can't really pray until we are
attentive to the business at hand—communion
with God. The one who thinks this is easy is in
for an awakening. Like a dog out in the field
at the beginning of the hunting season, our minds
go here, then there, now back, and off again. Don't
be alarmed. Bring your mind back as often as it
strays. Center down.

Stay put! In rural Mississippi we had a saying
that if a task was especially difficult it was accomplished *by main strength and awkwardness.*
Praying is like that—especially in its beginning.
Often the only way we stay with prayer is by main
strength and awkwardness. We have to *stay put*
for a set time in a set place in order to discipline
ourselves in attentiveness.

Wait for God! God is available. Though sometimes a hidden God, He is never a hiding God.
Sometimes we may not feel his presence. Our pre-

occupation with self may clog the line of communication. But wait! God is there. Take some time to be quiet and seek to be receptive. Remove, as far as is possible, the many considerations that clamor for our interest. Be done with the trivial matters that would keep us from being single-minded. Try to give God first place, even though you can't completely be free of these secondary thoughts. A prayer such as this, silently repeated, will help: "Here I am, Lord, in the stillness, waiting for thee."

We are well on the way when we realize that God was there first—and all the time—waiting for us. Don't miss the glory of this meeting.

Prayer: Here we are now, God, centered down, waiting for thee. Thou art here, though we may not know it. We are going to stay put until we realize thy presence. Amen.

Dull Habit or Acute Fever

> "Be careful for nothing; but in every thing by prayer and . . . thanksgiving let your requests be made known unto God."—Phil. 4:6 KJV

To his friend Donatus a Christian of the third century wrote a letter packed with unusual meaning. It was a remarkable testimony of the influence of Christ upon men of that day. "If I should ascend some high mountain, you know what I would see—armies fighting, brigands on the highway, pirates on the seas, men murdered in the amphitheater to please the applauding multitudes.

But in the midst of this I have found a quiet and holy people. They are persecuted, but they care not. They have found a joy a thousand times greater than any pleasure. These people are the masters of their own souls. They are the Christians, and I am one of them."

The writer was finally put to death, but the power of Christ was present in his life. The exhilarant joy of that unnamed Christian is glaringly missing today. William James said that religion in some exists as a dull habit, in others as an acute fever. Donatus' friend had the acute-fever type; ours is more a dull habit.

The religion which Jesus inspired and for which he died can never be a dull habit. From his prison in Rome Paul wrote the Philippians, "Be careful for nothing." That cancels out our prove-every-step approach to Christian living and serving, doesn't it? That's a red pencil line through the approach-it-with-caution philosophy that has characterized our devotional patterns.

"But in every thing by prayer and . . . thanksgiving let your requests be made known unto God." Here is the complete confidence that God will supply our needs. No reservations! Caution is cast to the wind. An almost wild abandonment typifies the instruction of Paul.

And how is it possible? How can our religious experience be transformed from "dull habit" into "acute fever"? Through a disciplined life of prayer —constant communion with God—we may recover the happy abandonment and quiet confidence that has always characterized the ardent Christian. A joy a thousand times greater than pleasure will radiate from us.

Margueritte Harmon Bro in *More Than We Are* has told the story of an old grandmother in Kansas whose life of devotion was a witness to this. Beginning the day she was married she read a Bible chapter every day. Whenever she found a promise she marked it with a "T" for *try*. As the years went by and the testing accumulated she marked a "P" for each promise proven. In her nineties her Bible was well marked, and she could proffer a book in which every promise bore her personal authentication "TP": the promises were tried and proven.

This is no dull habit we're talking about; it's an acute fever. Are you infected?

Prayer: We've reduced a thrilling experience to a dull habit, O Christ, and we repent. Forgive us now as we rise with a song and begin afresh the venture of faith. Amen.

The Single Eye

> "When thine eye is single, thy whole body also is full of light."—Luke 11:34 KJV

"It is the God-relationship that makes a man a man." Kierkegaard was talking about "the single eye." Until my relationship with God is settled I am not the man I was destined to be.

The basic principles of this relationship are *adoration* and *obedience*. On our knees we bow in adoration; on our feet we walk in service.

Zwingli told of a saintly woman who moved along the streets of Strasbourg with a flaming sword in one hand and a pail of water in the other. When questioned about the queer practice, she explained that with the torch she was going to burn the lovely furniture of heaven, and with the pail of water she was going to quench the fires of hell. Then, she said, people will love the Lord for himself alone, and not for the rewards of heaven or hell.

We can know that we are growing in the life of prayer when our selfish asking diminishes and we spend our prayer time primarily in adoration and praise.

There is no real separation of adoration and obedience. Adoration is the source of obedience and obedience feeds our adoration, preventing it from being empty and indulgent self-ecstasy. The words "worship" and "work" have the same root. Adoration results in adherence to God's will.

There is a rhythm here. Praise and service blend in a harmony. For once we begin to live in the presence of God, life becomes tremendously exciting. Emil Brunner says, "the Church exists by mission as fires exists by burning." The life of the *single eye* is like that. The fire of adoration burns in obedient service. A freedom hitherto unknown gives wings to our life. We are delivered from the frantic efforts of service and become open channels through which the love of God flows into the lives of others. We perform deliberate acts of compassion and concern, but no longer do these betray willful drudgery; they are smooth and natural, not stilted and determined.

"When thy eye is single, thy whole body also is full of light," Jesus said. This singleness of life comes from the marriage of adoration and obedience. The lives of the great artists illustrate this. Leonardo da Vinci sat patiently before the canvas on which he hoped to paint the picture of the Last Supper. In meditative waiting he sought the image of Christ within his mind. Wasting time! Doing nothing! Cheating his patrons! So people thought. But only out of that creative waiting came the masterpiece that thrills us yet.

In the Christian life it is the same. We seek a "single eye" that we might see things whole and that all life might be full of light. The time spent in adoration and praise is the fountain-head of the stream of obedient service that flows singingly from our lives into the lives of others.

Prayer: We would be single-minded in our devotion, O Christ. Thus we seek the "single eye" that our whole life may be full of light—thy light. Assist us in our quest. Amen.

The Harmony of Life

> "Bless the Lord, O my soul;
> and all that is within me, bless his holy name!"
> —Ps. 103:1 RSV

In the previous meditation we considered the "single eye"—the life that finds its light in the marriage of adoration and obedience. The psalmist was exulting in the joy of this wedding when he shouted,

> Bless the Lord, O my soul;
> and all that is within me, bless his holy name!"

The purpose of prayer is to unify life, to bring the fragments of our being together in a whole. Frank Laubach is one man in our age who has found this harmony. After spending some time in a conference with him, my wife wrote, "He is undoubtedly the greatest Christian I've ever met. When you talk to him he makes you feel like you are the only person around and you know he really loves you."

This has not always been the case with Dr. Laubach. He had failed in his missionary work with the fierce Moros Indians on the island of Mindanao in the Philippines. Discouraged, he cried out to God, "Why did you send me to this terrible place among these thieving, murdering, hateful people?" He found his answer in a disciplined life of devotion. On Signal Hill in back of his house where he spent much time in prayer, his despair was changed one night because his life was changed. Christ began to speak to him through his own lips, "Frank, they don't love you because you don't love them. You look down on them with your white man's sense of superiority. They read you like a book and they know that because you are educated as a Christian and as a white man you feel you are better than they are. If you would only love them they'd love you back."

That did it. Frank Laubach was transformed. From that point on he began to know the harmony of life. One of the great modern mystics, he is also one of the most vigorous servants of humanity, responsible for the literacy of millions, communicating love with a capacity unequaled in our day.

Here is the harmony of life—worship and work

blended, all of life made a sacrament. Our self-abandonment in the quiet places of our devotional life enables us to serve vigorously, creatively, and effectively in the streets and factories and offices of our daily living.

This harmony of life emerges from our sensitivity to God on the one hand, and our alertness to human need on the other. Sensitivity to God, cultivated through prayer, makes us susceptible to intimations from him and openness to his will. This, in turn, alerts us to the needs of the world and stimulates an active good will in all our relationships. This is a stream of love flowing in two directions—from my life to God and from my life outward to man. We are then enabled to convey God's love because we have received God's love. We learn that redemptive action on our part is dependent upon a selfless devotion to the purposes of Divine Love.

Prayer: We want to bless thee, O Lord, with our whole being. In our quiet time and at our job, may all that is within us bless thy holy name. Amen.

DEVELOPMENT

Be Babies No Longer

> "Until we all attain to the unity of the faith and of the knowledge of the Son of God, to mature manhood, to the measure of the stature of the fullness of Christ."—Eph. 4:13 RSV

It has been suggested that one of the simplest ways to gain insight into another person is to see what he underlines as he reads. We read with our needs.

If this is true we can discover the need of our generation. Underlined more than once, in all that we have been reading, is the word "maturity." It stands out in bold relief.

This is as it should be. We ought to be deeply engaged in an inquiry about ourselves as persons.

What makes us whole? What gives us fulfillment?

André Maurois, a literary critic, has said, "Almost all the great novels have as their motif, more or less disguised, the passage from childhood to maturity, the clash between the thrill of expectation and a disillusioning knowledge of truth." Does this not pinpoint the meaning of life?—a journey from childhood to maturity.

Amazingly, this was a preoccupation with Paul in the New Testament. He wrote to the church at Ephesus a word strangely modern in its application. We must not be babies any longer, blown about and swung around by every wind. . . . We must lovingly hold to the truth and grow up into perfect union with Christ himself (Eph. 4:14-15). And again, as he brought his magnificent hymn of love (I Cor. 13) to a close he sounded this note: "When I was a child, I spoke like a child, I thought like a child, I understood like a child; when I became a man, I gave up childish ways" (vs. 11 RSV). Here he emphasizes the fact that love demands maturity for its full flowering.

Colloquial speech has performed a real service in calling an untested, merely romantic relationship between a man and a woman or a boy and a girl "puppy love." In all our understanding we need maturity. How we need maturity in our understanding of love and its meaning!

Herman Melville, in his novel *Pierre,* sourly defines the gospel of love as "a volume bound in rose-leaves, clasped with violets, and by the beaks of hummingbirds printed with peach-juice on the leaves of lilies." This is a blasphemous definition of a way of life which led Jesus to the cross and has demanded the lifeblood of thousands. And yet many of us have not matured beyond this point in our understanding of love. We are always thinking in terms of gooey sentimentalism, loving everybody in general and no one in particular; thinking of problems far removed from us, but never applying mature love to the basic relationships of life. In fact, most of us are not willing to think conscientiously and study seriously the implications of Christian love, which is love at its highest.

The future demands such a consideration. We can be babies no longer, "blown about and swung around by every wind." We must become men in our spiritual life; we must mature in our understanding. We have been under the disastrous illusion that Christianity is a religion for children and not for adults. Perhaps this is the one thing that is damning any conscientious program of redemption and service on the part of the Christian church. We have within our churches too many people whose religious experience amounts to a few memories of Sunday school. This is not adequate for the storms of later life. It certainly isn't sufficient for a society of people with "no principles in an easy world."

"When I became a man, I gave up childish ways." "We must not be babies any longer, blown about and swung around by every wind. . . . We must lovingly hold to the truth and grow up into perfect union with Christ himself." By study, prayer, discussion, discipline—and all the ways a person matures, we must seek maturity in love. When we have matured here, we are babies no longer, but are developing into true manhood.

97

Prayer: Above all things, our Christ, keep us mindful of our need to grow—especially to grow in love. Amen.

Love, Not Legalism

> "Anything you did for one of my brothers here, however humble, you did for me."—Matt. 25: 40 NEB

Continue your thinking about love. Jesus' primary method of teaching was by parable. When he wanted to convey a profound truth, he told a story. One of his most pointed is the story of the last judgment when the sheep would be separated from the goats. Syrian sheep were usually white, and Syrian goats were usually black. When the combined flock came together at night the shepherd could separate them without mistake, even in the dusk. Jesus said that with the same sureness the Eternal God would judge mankind. Men would be separated as the shepherd separated the sheep from the goats.

We don't like that, do we? It's altogether too specific! We want to protest. How can judgment be so sure? There is so much good in the worst of us, and so much bad in the best of us; human character moves back and forth through so many different shades of gray. But Jesus drew a line clear through the middle of humanity. And the line is not where we usually think it to be. No rules and regulations, no niceties to which we conform, no certain creeds to which we adhere, no particular ritual or liturgy that we have to accept and parrot—

our judgment, the judgment of humanity, would be based on our love, our concern, our active sympathy for others. And again, "anything you did *not* for one of these, however humble, you did *not* for me." There is the basis for judgment.

The love, or lack of love in a man's life—this is the determining factor. Did Jesus not spell it out in bold letters? When a young lawyer asked him the secret of life, Jesus returned the question, "What is the commandment?" Then the young scribe recited with assurance, "Thou shalt love the Lord thy God with all thy heart—and thy neighbor as thyself." With finality Jesus said, "This do and you shall live." Love for God and love for man— this is good religion in action.

Do you remember the story of Martin of Tours? He was a Roman soldier and a Christian. One cold winter day, as he was entering a city, a beggar stopped him and asked him for alms. Martin had no money, but he gave what he did have. The beggar was blue and shivering with cold. Though it was worn and frayed, Martin took off his soldier's coat and cut it in two, giving half of it to the beggar man. That night he had a dream. In it he had a vision of heaven; the angels were there with Jesus in the midst of them. He was wearing half a Roman soldier's coat. One of the angels asked him, "Master, why are you wearing that battered old coat? Who gave it to you?" And Martin heard Jesus answer softly, "My servant, Martin, gave it to me."

It may be an apocryphal story, but we don't miss the point, do we? "Anything you did for one of my brothers, however humble, you did for me." Love . . . that you might be called children of the Father.

Love, not legalism, is at the heart of good religion, and especially Christianity. If you want to know how you are coming along in religious growth examine yourself against this principle.

Prayer: Free us, Father, from the stifling chains of legalism. Enable us to love—spontaneously. Amen.

Synthetic Brains and Cybernetics

> "And God said, Let us make man in our image . . . and let them have dominion."
> —Gen. 1:26 KJV

Inexpensive, easily manufactured, electronic "synthetic brains"! This is what Simon Ramo, president of the Bunker-Ramo Corporation called for in delivering the keynote address before the National Symposium on the Impact of Batch Fabrication on Future Computers.

Dr. Ramo made it clear that he was not asking that man try to duplicate the human brain. The idea was to combine and mesh the best of both systems—the general flexibility of the natural brain with the narrow specialist problem-solving ability of electronic components.

In other developments discussions go on as to the place of the computer in every area of life. One of the most fascinating discussions has to do with the computer as a servant of research in the arts. At a conference on "The Computer in Musical Research and Composition" sponsored by UCLA-IBM, it was concluded that while computers are not likely to produce a Mozart or a Beethoven, they can certainly be an aid to the composer.

When we read such reports as these we thrill at the advancement of man. His technological achievements make even science fiction that appeared wild ten years ago tame in comparison.

Rare is the person who will question even the wildest dreams of the possibilities of man. If Shakespeare lived today, would he add any words to his lines of praise? "What a piece of work is a man! how noble in reason! how infinite in faculty! in form and moving how express and admirable! in action how like an angel! in apprehension how like a god!"

All sorts of questions are raised when synthetic brains and cybernetics are contemplated. What role will the computer play in man's moral decisions? Will some electronic device be employed in choosing a wife? Will cybernetics replace the demands of adequate human relations? Will the machine do away with man's ethical responsibility? Interesting questions, aren't they?

The glory of man is not seen though in a synthetic brain or a mind-staggering computer. Man is more than that which he creates, and far more than mechanistic reflexes. Stanton A. Coblentz has some lines entitled "A Materialist Pictures Man" which speaks to us here.

He showed the skin, and thought to show the man;
Charted each bone and muscle, nerve and vein.
And only these were missing from the plan:
The heart, the soul, the brain.

The machine can never be superior to the man who creates it. The computer is always dependent upon the information fed to it by man, and the answers it provides are always assimilated and used by man. So man is still the master.

At times we may be overpowered by all these developments. We may tend to feelings of inferiority. But remember who you are! Synthetic brains, however highly developed, are always developed by real brains. Computers, however spectacular in efficiency, are our servants, not our masters. Man, not the machine, can glory in a sunset and write a sonnet about it. Only man can know and give love at its highest. Only man can commune with God and respond to his intimations. Keeping this fresh in our minds we can develop into the "little-lower-than-the-angels" creatures God intended us to be.

Prayer: Eternal God, as thy creatures we are less than thee, our Creator; keep us mindful that the works of our minds and hands are less than we. Thus may we "have dominion." Amen.

The Road and the Inn

> "For he was looking forward to the city with firm foundations, whose architect and builder is God."—Heb. 11:10 NEB

"The road is always better than the inn." These words of Cervantes, the Spanish writer, suggests a way of living. Unfortunately, most of us prefer the inn to the road. We fail to realize that the inn is only a resting place where we can be refreshed and strengthened for the road again.

How many times have you set a goal for yourself, worked hard for its achievement only to find that this was not an inn at which you could settle down and stay forever; it was only a point along the road that continued on?

The inn is necessary, but the road is more important. The real excitement of life comes from the road itself. Kahlil Gibran wrote of this:

> Happiness is a myth we seek,
>   If manifested surely irks;
> Like river speeding to the plain,
>   On its arrival slows and murks.
>
> For man is happy only in
>   His aspiration to the heights;
> When he attains his goal, he cools
>   And longs for distant flights.
>   —"Of Happiness and Hope"

Satisfaction and reward are not at the inn, but along the road.

Recently I talked with two men about retirement. One man had this advice to offer: "Learn to play now. Develop recreational outlets and hobbies that you will enjoy when you have time on your hands." The other said, "Don't ever retire!" Both were saying something about the road and the inn. Many look to retirement as an inn to which they will come and forever "take their ease." For many this becomes a drudgery rather than a dream of fulfillment. Life was never meant to stop abruptly at some inn of doing-nothing. Some people can make that kind of adjustment, but most can't. We need to be prepared to continue the journey in some sort of creative pursuits. Our movement may not be at the same rapid pace. To be sure, we ought to "slow down." But settling down in the inn is not the answer.

When a person comes to the point in life when he can't look to the future, life is over. This has nothing to do with physical age. It has to do with outlook, with faith and hope. A man of seventy can face the future with a traveler's stride, even as a man of thirty. At our best and at every point along the way we ought to know that we are going somewhere.

Jesus began his parable of the talents with these words: "For the kingdom of heaven is as a man travelling" (Matt. 25:14 KJV). Gerald Kennedy has suggested that "there is a sense in which that broken sentence expresses a complete truth. We cannot long stay content with a way of life that does not change. When we come to a dead end, that is cause for despair. We cannot long endure without faith in tomorrow, and we cannot keep our spirits alive unless we can look to the future with hope. I believe that men cannot long live without faith in a final plan and purpose in life."

The inn is not a stopping point, but a starting place for some new endeavor. The pace will change and the goals will be different, but the road will be there, the road of life, and we'll know that we ought to walk it. "The road is always better than the inn."

Prayer: The city is ahead of us, our Father. There are inns along the way and we enjoy the re-creation they afford. But enable us to stay on the road with eyes focused on the future. Amen.

The Mountains and Plains of Life

> "Every valley shall be exalted . . . and the crooked shall be made straight, and the rough places plain."—Isa. 40:4 KJV

Snoopy, the sometimes-more-than-human dog in Charles Schulz's comic strip *Peanuts,* had been rather happy for several days. But then his mood changed. He was downcast. Dejected and sad, he listened to a lecture from Linus who was seeking to cheer him up.

"You really can't expect to be happy all the time," Linus said. "You're bound to have ups and downs. . . . It's only human! If you'll pardon the expression."

It *is* only human, isn't it? Life is that way. There are the mountains and the plains, the peaks of glory and the valleys of despair. We have felt with Wordsworth

> A presence that disturbs me with the joy
> Of elevated thoughts;

We have also known with Wordsworth the despair of his confession:

> I lost
> All feeling of conviction, and . . .
> . . . .
> Yielded up moral questions in despair.

This seems to be the way life is ordered. There are the high moments and the low, the shimmering peaks of inspiration and the pensive plains of loneliness, the brilliant glow of discovered glory and the gloomy shadows of sorrow, the ecstasy of heavenly communion and the dreary monotony of work-a-day living, the surge of unleased moral power and the impotence of apathy and unconcern.

The sooner we recognize this the better: we can never have the mountains without the valley. In fact, the mountains were made for the valley. "All sunshine makes a desert," so goes the wise proverb. We shouldn't expect to experience the mountain always.

The most victorious life ever lived, Jesus of Nazareth, showed the rhythmic balance between the mountain and the plain. If anyone should have expected to live on the heights he should. But even he could never do it. "Now is my soul troubled. . . . Father, save me from this hour." (John 12:27 KJV.) That was a day of mist and fog. But there were even more crucial times: "My God, my God, why hast thou forsaken me?" Jesus knew the valley.

Likewise you and me. We are going to have our valleys and plains—and we ought to. But here is the glory of it: if we have been to the mountain, and if we have gained the great spiritual resources that are available there, we need not worry about the plains. They, too, will be avenues of growth and development.

Roy DeLamotte tells of visiting an elderly little lady whose life story is an inspiration here. Her body was bowed by a lifetime of labor and trouble.

She spoke of entering the textile mill as a child laborer, so small she carried a box to stand on. The few cents an hour she received for an eleven-hour day went to a hard-drinking father, and her only comprehension of a strike was that it was a chance for her and the other children to run and play outdoors. Her thin voice poured out the ancient story of a brutal and unimaginative social system which had clearly blighted in her any shoots of personality we might consider cultural or creative. But toward the close of her little life history, the tired voice took on a peaceful vitality and warmth as she spoke of climbing the stairs in childhood to her attic room. There above the stultifying drudgery of a mill village and hidden from the eye of a drunken father and an uninterested stepmother, she communed with a different and a fairer world. The sad face softened and the sinewy hands relaxed as she concluded,

"And God was with me, all the way."

This has always been the supreme experience life affords. When we walk through the lowest plains and the darkest valleys, when we know "the little days of our lives fly swifter than a weaver's shuttle," we can know there is another world, we can know that there is a mountain peak to which we can go, and there in communion with God we can be renewed and transformed. We can then walk back to the plains, standing erect, striding triumphantly, confident and courageous.

The mountains and the plains of life are inevitable. It's how we handle them that counts!

Prayer: Give us the grace, our Father, to turn the plains of our experience into opportunities for development. Enable us to carry with us from the mountains to the plains the resources by which this might be done. Through Christ our Lord. Amen.

Not What We Live With, *but What We Live* For

> "Foxes have holes, and the birds of the air have
> nests; but the Son of man hath not where to lay
> his head."—Matt. 8:20 KJV

Outward conditions are the convenient excuses we use to hang our inner failures. If things do not go as they should, we were hampered by the circumstances. If we miss the mark in life, it was fate that did it. When the roll of history is called, such excuses are seen for what they are—*excuses*.

The important matter is not what we have to live *with*, but what we live *for*. No one has illustrated this more dramatically than Viktor E. Frankl in his lucid account of three grim years at Auschwitz and other Nazi prisons, as found in his *Man's Search for Meaning*.

We who lived in concentration camps can remember the men who walked through the huts comforting others, giving away their last piece of bread. They may have been few in number, but they offer sufficient proof that everything can be taken from a man but one thing: the last of the human freedoms—to choose one's attitude in any given set of circumstances, to choose one's own way.

And there were always choices to make. Every day, every hour, offered the opportunity to make a decision, a decision which determined whether you would or would not submit to those powers which threatened to rob you of your very self, your inner freedom; which determined whether or not you would become the plaything of circumstance, renouncing freedom and dignity to become molded into the form of the typical inmate.

Development in the Christian life is especially dependent upon our recognition of this. We may not control the circumstances of life, but we can control their effect upon us.

I'm thinking now of a person in our community with whom I recently visited. It is difficult for some to imagine that a person with such limited means, living in such dire circumstances, could be found in our affluent little city. But she is here. Her monthly income is $107. Of this she pays $55 for a two-room apartment, leaving only $52 for food, clothing, and other basic essentials. For the first time during the two years I had known her, I found her depressed. She apologized for the chilly room and her obvious distress. She had had little food and no money for two weeks. The tight lines on her brow relaxed and her strained face softened as we began to talk and as she shared some of her recent involvements in service to others. Before I left she showed me a little coat and two dresses she had purchased at Goodwill Industries with money she could ill afford to spend. They were gifts for some Negro children she had come to love while working with Operation Head Start the previous summer.

From where does her usual happiness and well-being derive? Not from outward circumstances, but from inner resources which she has cultivated. What she has to live *for*—her commitment to Christ and her concern for others—not what she has to live *with*, is the fountainhead of her development in the Christian life.

Prayer: Loving Father, excuses have helped us none. We are tired of making them. We want to use our circumstances rather than allowing them to use us. Give us strength. Amen.

Overcoming Circumstances

> "For I know that this shall turn to my salvation through your prayer, and the supply of the Spirit of Jesus Christ."—Phil. 1:19 KJV

In the previous meditation we examined the truth that it is not what we live *with,* but what we live *for* that is important. To recognize this truth is necessary, but it is not enough.

I can hear one say, "So what we live with is not so important as what we live for. But where do I go from here? I've turned my eyes inward but have not found the power about which you speak." This is not unusual—especially for the person who has only recently embarked upon the Way, or the one who has not been serious in efforts at growth in the Christian life.

We look within and find a blank. No power there! Why? We have not developed the inner resources of energy. We have externalized our search for meaning. The notion that happiness consists of what we possess has dominated our quest. We can't shake the idea that our inner well-being is in someway tied to our outward circumstances. Such a search terminates in the pillbox —$150,000,000 spent annually on tranquilizers.

We can overcome outward circumstances only as we develop these inner resources through a life of prayer and devotion discussed in another section. Madame Guyon found the secret. She was a mystic, a friend of the great Fenelon, an enthusiastic apostle of Quietism. After an unhappy marriage and the eventual death of her husband who had been the victim of a long illness, she started her career as an evangelist of Quietism. As her influence expanded she incurred the displeasure of the Roman Catholic Church and persecution began. After a series of imprisonments and continuous refusal to cease her preaching, she was incarcerated in the Bastille from 1698 to 1702, expecting every day to be executed for heresy. After her release she was banished to a distant province and there lived with her daughter in retirement. The tribulations of her outward circumstances never crushed her spirit. Her center was not in these outward circumstances, but within. So she could write

> My Lord, how full of sweet content
> I pass my years of banishment!
> Wher'er I dwell, I dwell with thee,
> In Heaven, in earth, or on the sea.

As with Madame Guyon, we overcome outward circumstances with inner resources developed through prayer. When we make a habit of sincere prayer, our lives are profoundly altered. A steady flow of power floods our lives and works a quiet miracle. This is not only a transforming power, but a sustaining one. We can then look within to find the strength to overcome all adversity.

Prayer: We are on the way, our Father, seeking to develop the inner resources of our life. Enable us to be constant in our efforts, overcoming as we go. Amen.

DIVIDENDS

We Get What We Want

> "Delight thyself also in the Lord; and he shall give thee the desires of thine heart."—Psalm 37:4 KJV

One ship drives east and another drives west
 With the selfsame winds that blow.
   'Tis the set of the sails
   And not the gales
 Which tells us the way to go.
   —Ella Wheeler Wilcox, "The Winds of Fate"

Have you noted it? We always get what we want—don't we? We always end up at our desired destination—don't we?

Your immediate response is negative. "If I got what I wanted I wouldn't be slaving in the humdrum job that I have," you say. "If I had my desires I wouldn't be living in the cramped quarters that my family has long since outgrown." "I wouldn't be playing second fiddle to a boss that

112

is calloused and overbearing." "If I got what I wanted I certainly wouldn't be in the shape I am in today." "If my desires were satisfied I wouldn't have to pinch pennies and worry about bills."

Though all the responses may be true, there is something deeper and far more significant. There is a force that propels our lives in whatever direction we are going. We live the kind of lives we live and we reap our rewards of good and evil, all according to that for which we most deeply hunger.

Any minister who has to talk long to the troubled souls that beat a pathway to his study door soon comes to realize that deep within every troubled soul there are dark, hidden, and oftentimes unconscious forces that have brought the misery that is tormenting the individual now seeking escape. The ancients thought man had no choice in these forces that directed his life. In Sophocles' famous play, *Oedipus Rex*, Oedipus' parents tried to avoid the fate the gods had decreed for their young, beloved son. A bleak destiny awaited him. It would be his lot, the gods said, to murder his father and marry his mother. Confronted with that destiny, the parents were advised to kill their son while he was still a little child so that he could avoid such a repulsive end. A faithful servant took the lad into the woods, but, rather than kill him, he bound him and left him to die.

He was discovered by an old shepherd and nursed to maturity—not knowing who he was. In the end, however, Oedipus stands before the people of Thebes, the great city over which he had come to rule, to discover to his horror that what "Nemesis" (fate) had designed for him had been accomplished. Something over which he had

113

had no control compelled Oedipus, against his will, to the destiny of his birth. He had killed his father and married his mother.

Unadmittedly, many of us have found consolation in such a philosophy. "It's in the stars," we say. Now the figure is changed: "It's all in the cards." Many of us are not willing to admit that we have a role to play in our destiny.

It is everlastingly true. History has proved it; personal biography affirms it; all the forces of the universe point to it. We get what we want. *We determine our dividends.*

Remember now, we are not talking about the surface desires of our life. We are talking about the deep "set of the soul." When the light dawns upon us, we realize, even amidst our whining, that the ship of our life comes into the harbor we have chosen. The set of our soul brings it there.

Examine your wants. Keep a close tab on them. For what you want most you are sure to get!

Prayer: Enable us, O God, to discipline ourselves to desire the highest, knowing that what we want we will get. Amen.

We Don't Want What We Get

> "All things are full of labour; man cannot utter it: the eye is not satisfied with seeing, nor the ear filled with hearing. . . . All is vanity and vexation of spirit."—Ecc. 1:8, 14 KJV

One of the great facts of life, as we discussed above, is that we get what we want.

This is a strange truth. But here is stranger yet: *We don't want what we get.*

An ancient Greek myth, which has been made into a fairy tale, will illustrate the truth. Midas, a king of Phrygia, succeeded in obtaining from the god Dionysus the promise that he would grant him his most overpowering wish. Thoughtfully, Midas considered what he wanted most of all. Then it came to him: he asked for the golden touch, that everything he touched would turn to gold. The wish was granted, and Midas was happy —for a little while.

Quickly he amassed a fortune. Being an unselfish fellow, so he thought, he planned a lavish banquet to which he invited his friends. He wanted to share his good fortune with them.

Then came the irony. As he began to eat, the meat became only gold as he touched it. The rich red wine he loved so well became a stream of liquid gold. Dismayed at this unexpected result of his power, Midas was momentarily rescued from his despair when he saw his little daughter, whom he loved so dearly, rushing toward him with open arms. He clasped her to his breast and she turned to gold in his arms.

He had destroyed the thing he loved most of all. He got what he wanted but discovered he didn't want what he got. He had to beg Dionysus to take his favor back.

It is only a myth, you say. Yet, Midas' experience is duplicated a million times over in life. Getting what we want, we find that we really don't want it.

Think. How many things have you worked hard for, desired with all your being, dedicated your energies and talents to—only to find that when you got it, when it was finally your own, it was like dust in your hand? Oh, you were happy for a season. You knew satisfaction for a time. But it was short-lived. It ended and you had to start over again in some other direction.

The mournful confession of the author of the book of Ecclesiastes is an honest one. He tried everything in life, he tells us: pleasure, religion, money; you name it, he tried it. The tragic testimony he bore at the end of his life was a pathetic commentary on many of our lives: *"Therefore I hated life . . . for all is vanity and vexation of spirit"* (2:17 KJV).

An Austrian journalist, reporting in the July 7, 1962, issue of the *Saturday Review,* his impression of a visit to the United States, makes a similar assessment of our situation in America. He finds that American people are running out of interesting things to do or think about. He says they have no real feeling of involvement in the nation or the world, except as it may affect their earning power. In particular, he says that American wives are liberated from everything, including purpose and a sense of responsibility. They make an occupation of being decorative. They are expensive, self-centered, demanding, complicated, vestigial. As for the husbands, he claims that so much male energy goes into pyramiding their business holdings that very little is left for family life and almost none for vital issues.

Now, the journalist could be wrong. In fact, he emphasizes that his impressions are purely personal and lack the comprehensive evidence that would be required for a sociological survey. Scientific or not, I join him in observing that we in

America are victims of a "lavish drift." We go from one thing to another, getting what we want, but once we get it, it isn't what we wanted at all.

What is the problem? Here it is: *Nothing ever pleases a man who is not pleased with himself.* Nothing outside a person, no matter what it is: fame, fortune, name, it doesn't matter; nothing outside a person is going to bring satisfaction to a person who is not satisfied *inside.* Ultimate satisfaction comes from within, not without.

Prayer: "Set our feet on lofty places." Guide us in the right direction, O God, for we know that we will arrive some day. We want to arrive at the right place. Amen.

Revealing Statistics

> "It is my prayer that your love may abound more and more, with knowledge and all discernment, so that you may approve what is excellent."—Phil. 1:9-10 RSV

As in life so in death Marilyn Monroe was under the public microscope. She left behind the same mysterious personality contrast that she evinced in life. When I read of her death, an interview with this movie star a few years ago came to my mind. The interviewer asked her how she would like to be remembered on her tombstone. She suggested her epitaph in these words: Marilyn Monroe; Blond; 37-23-36.

I read this account and the comments on her death. "No notes were found. She was found lying face down, the covers hunched around her shoulders. The body was taken to a nearby mortuary and then to the county morgue where it remains today, unclaimed. Hours before she had been one of the world's most famous personalities. But on her coroner's call sheet, tagged to crypt 33 in the morgue, were these unrevealing statistics: Weight 117 pounds, height 65½ inches, hair blonde and eyes blue. Next of kin—Gladys Baker, mother, address unknown."

Then the writer made this comment: "She seemed happy as Marilyn Monroe, the star, with the spotlights beaming brightly. But when the lights went off in her lonely bedroom, Marilyn Monroe, the sex symbol, was Norma Jean Baker, lost waif in a lost world."

There must be something we can learn from all this. We ought to learn that somewhere along the way we have lost our sense of values. Marilyn Monroe made more money in one movie than an average schoolteacher earns in twenty-five years.

We should learn also that life is made up in its ultimate meaning not of the lights of the world that shine upon it, or the plaudits of men, but of that which radiates from life to affect men and the world.

Above all we should learn that when life has no deep and abiding purpose to guide it, when it has no high and noble cause to serve, it grows dull on our hands and will eventually wither away. The unrevealing statistics of Marilyn Monroe were really revealing. They revealed a life that had grown lifeless in the midst of what so many think is real life. Contemplate again that haunting word of the news writer: "She seemed happy as

Marilyn Monroe, the star, with the spotlights beaming brightly. But when the lights went off in her lonely bedroom, Marilyn Monroe, the sex symbol, was Norma Jean Baker, lost waif in a lost world."

Will we learn from this? The dividends of a life that has no deep and abiding purpose to guide it, that has no high and noble cause to serve, are dullness and meaninglessness. Such a life wilts on our hands and will eventually wither away.

Prayer: Give us a sense of what is vital, our Father. May we not come to the end of life stunned by the fact we have not really lived. Amen.

Hatred Is a Boomerang

> "Do not let the sun go down on your anger."
> —Eph. 4:26 RSV

Hatred is one of the most destructive of all emotions. It is like a boomerang; it always comes back to hurt the one who flings it.

The man who harbors hatred in his heart is the man who suffers. We can hate others and plan our revenge; we can design our plots against them— even if these plots come off, hatred will never work as much harm to the one we hate as it will to us. Like a boomerang, it is sure to hit you harder than the fellow you throw it at. Hating, then, is like burning down our own houses to get rid of the rats.

Booker T. Washington was walking down a street with a white friend when he was roughly elbowed into the gutter by a passing pedestrian.

His friend was furious, exclaiming, "How can you tolerate such an insult?" Washington replied, "I defy any man to make me hate."

That has always been an inspiration to me. I get a good bit of anonymous mail. Sometimes it is a hate sheet. Again, it will be an envelope stuffed with "letters to the editor" or editorials that my unknown correspondent thinks have relevance to me. In every case they are scathingly bitter. I have determined that I will not allow this resentment to enter my mind. So, I open each envelope, look at the material, then pray for the person who sent it. Who knows? In a mysterious way known only to God the senders are going to be helped by these prayers. Also, I find it a good spiritual discipline because it frees me of the bitterness that could be harbored against those "anonymous haters."

I have heard that in Polynesia it is customary for the natives to keep reminders of their hatred. This is the reason so much time is spent in fighting. Articles are suspended from the ceiling of the house to keep alive the memory of the wrongs. Each night as a man goes to bed he looks up and is reminded of his hate; each morning as he wakes up he is reminded again.

We do not have these objects of reminder in our homes, perhaps, but many of us have our shrines of hate. If we attend these shrines too often, we will ruin our lives. Man was not made to hate. Paul offered sound advice, "Do not let the sun go down on your anger." For hatred we must substitute love.

Upon the marsh mud, dank and foul,
A golden sunbeam softly fell,

And from the noisome depths arose
  A lily miracle.

Upon a dark bemired life
  A gleam of human love was flung,
And lo, from that ungenial soil
  A noble life upsprung.
            —L. M. Montgomery, "Love's Miracle"

Hatred is destructive; love is creative. Why not make the substitution?

Prayer: "O divine Master, grant that I may not so much seek to be consoled as to console; to be understood, as to understand; to be loved, as to love; for it is in giving that we receive; it is in pardoning that we are pardoned; and it is in dying that we are born to eternal life." (Francis of Assisi)

In Quest of a Thrill

**"My heart and flesh sing for joy
to the living God."—Ps. 84:2 RSV**

"We did it for kicks!"

This is what two young fellows told me not long ago when they were caught by the police taking cases of coke bottles from a drive-in cafe. I don't know what these fellows would have done with the bottles—sell them, I suppose—but they didn't need the money. Their indifferent reply to my inquiries was, "We did it for kicks."

In recent times in many of our cities, teenagers from some of the most socially and economically prominent families have gone on tirades of cutting

121

automobile tires and slicing convertible tops. When the judge questioned them, they only replied to the effect that they were "looking for a thrill."

This story is repeated over and over again. From throwing toilet tissue on people's lawns to wild racing in automobiles that have been given to them much too early, young people are *out for kicks.*

It is not restricted to youth. Look around you at the adult population. Examine your own weekly activities. How many crazy things do you do and find others doing "just for kicks," "looking for a thrill"?

Could it be that religion has failed at this point?

What an exciting thing to read the eighty-fourth psalm in this relation. The psalmist is literally singing with joy. Here is a positive, exhilarant mood which cannot be mistaken. Here is the song of gladness of a man who has experienced the blessing of communion with God. Listen to him:

> "My heart and flesh sing for joy
> to the living God."

What a testimony to a people who have allowed their religion to be reduced to a few irrelevant prohibitions and a dusty code of conduct that was outmoded long before the horse and buggy went out of style! What a challenge to the dull, matter-of-fact, take-it-or-leave-it routine that passes for religion in some quarters. To a generation whose activities have been directed in quest of a thrill, we have offered a pallid form of religion that misses not only the experience of this psalmist, but also, of course, the dominant note of the New Testament: *joy and confidence.*

An age of insecurity has made us a breathless, bewildered people. We look for the thrills aplenty which this nervous age affords. Oh, for the exhilarating experience of the psalmist: "Now soul and body thrill with joy over the living God" (Moffatt).

This is the thrill our guilt-ridden, nervous, uneasy age needs: a steady confidence in the living God, the relief and freedom of Christian love and forgiveness, the assurance of grace and fellowship in the Christian community. When this experience is ours, not only will we thrill with joy, we will thrill others.

Prayer: Our Father, may our experience of thee be so full and complete that our spirit will contagiously radiate the thrill of our religion. Amen.

Surprised by Joy

> "And when he saw their faith he said, 'Man, your sins are forgiven you.' "—Luke 5:20 RSV

C. S. Lewis calls his autobiography *Surprised by Joy*. To him the astounding effect of the Christian gospel was the joy which he found in it. This was all unlooked for. He never expected what he found when he finally received and accepted the gospel.

This is always the case even though it continues to amaze us. Robert Luccock reminds us that in these three words Lewis describes the effect which the gospel always has on people who accept it. They are "surprised by joy."

123

Consider this familiar story in the New Testament. There was an independent, adventurous young man who grew tired of the provincial village in which he lived and the monotonous life on the farm. He decided to get away from it all, so he claimed his inheritance early and went into a far country where he squandered his life away. When his wanton waste and extravagance brought the decadence of the pig pen, he began to think of his father's home and how even all the hired help had it better than he. Coming to his senses, he decided to go home again—not as a son but as a servant. Laden with the burden of sin and remorse, he started out, wondering all the way how he would be received. He was putting the finishing polish on his much rehearsed speech of confession, far down the road from his house, when he was "surprised by joy." His father had been looking for him. Seeing him far, far down the road, he ran to him, threw his arms around him, and kissed him. You know the unimagined joy of the young man, the party that followed, and the hilarious reception of the fellow back into the father's fold.

So it is today. Here again, we are always surprised by joy. Full of remorse, sick of sin, wanting to be back home in the Father's house, wanting to be reconciled as children of God, and never knowing just how it shall be, we are met with the forgiveness of God.

Nothing is more needed in our day than this wonderful "surprise of God." At one time or another most of us are aware of this tremendous need—the need of forgiveness. The forgiveness God affords is always a surprise. Alec Vidler in

Christian Belief suggests that it is something like this:

A tradesman in a certain town found that one of his trusted men had been systematically stealing from his warehouse for years. Some people might have been soft and let him off the punishment, which is a kind of indulgence that modern men profess to admire though they seldom practise it themselves. Other people would have been hardboiled and would have cast the culprit adrift. But this man's employer did neither the one nor the other. He let him be tried and sentenced and sent to prison. But when the man came out of prison his employer was there to greet him with the words, "Your place is open for you; come back, we will start afresh." And when the man reached home, he found that his wages had been paid in full to his wife all the time he had been in prison. He was punished; but he was forgiven, and creatively forgiven. The forgiveness of God is like that.

When we are filled with remorse and know that the only desert for our sins is the condemnation of God, when we know that if justice prevailed we would deserve eternal death, we are "surprised by joy." God meets us and draws us unto himself and restores us to our place of fellowship in Christian communion.

This doesn't mean that we won't suffer. The sinner always suffers. For every sin there is a cost. God doesn't set the cost; he doesn't demand that a penalty be paid. This is the law of life. But the glory of it is that by "his stripes are we healed." He turns our darkness into light by forgiveness and the "prodigal" can come home. We are "surprised by joy."

Prayer: In thy forgiveness we find joy, O loving Father. May that joy continue to flow. Amen.

The Grandest Surprise

"In my Father's house are many mansions." —John 14:2 KJV

Everyone likes surprises. There is the simple delight, even in adults, that comes when we are taken off guard by some unanticipated act of appreciation and love. Consider the grandest surprise of all. Mary Magdalene is walking in the garden in the early hours of the morning in deep despair. The mist that preceded the coming dawn only hinted at the mist that veiled her heart. She is there to see where they have buried Jesus. When she doesn't find him, she asks the gardener where they have taken him. The gardener speaks just one word, her name, "Mary," and the unbelievable surprise of the Resurrection floods over her soul.

This is God's ultimate surprise. It is the Mt. Everest of Christian experience—to be surprised by the meaning of the Resurrection. Even an agnostic such as Robert Ingersoll would express longing for this surprise. Standing at the grave of his brother, he said, "Life is a narrow veil between the cold and barren peaks of two eternities. We strive to look beyond their heights. We cry aloud, and the only answer is the echo of our wailing cry. But hope sees a star, and in the night of death, listening love can hear the rustle of an angel's wings."

This is not enough! We need more than a faint hope that enables us to hear the "rustle of an angel's wings." All of us are caught up in the agony of bereavement at one time or another. A loved one is taken from us, and the question of what lies beyond clamors persistently for an answer.

This is where God so wonderfully surprises us. Those who live by the Christian faith are never left to this agonizing plight, and we can affirm Sunday after Sunday, "I believe in the resurrection of the body, and the life everlasting."

The Yearling, by Marjorie Kinnan Rawlings, has a picture of the certainty that is ours. One of the moving scenes comes at the funeral of Fodder-wing, the pitiful, crippled, half-wit boy in the story. This child with twisted body and twisted mind had a way with animals. Amazingly, all the little wild creatures became his friends. When Fodder-wing died, his body was placed in a rough handmade casket. Even though no preacher was among them the family and friends gathered for a funeral and their minds inevitably turned to God in the mystery of death. One of them turned to Penny, the one character in the book who stands out and stays clean in the midst of the primitive surroundings and hardships, and said, "Penny, you've had Christian raising. We'd be proud, did you say somethin'." Penny stood at the open grave and lifting his face to the sunlight while the rough men bowed their heads, he offered his prayer:

O Lord. Almighty God. Hit ain't for us ignorant mortals to say what's right and what's wrong. Was ary one of us to be a'doin' of it, we'd not of brung this pore boy into the world a cripple, and his mind teched. We'd of brung him in straight and tall like his brothers, fitten to live and work and do. But in a way o' speakin', Lord, you done made it up to him. . . . You give him a sort o' wisdom, made him knowin' and gentle. The birds come to him and the varmints moved free about him, and like as not he could o' takened a she wild cat right in his pore twisted hands.

Now you've done seed fit to take him where bein' crookedy in mind or limb don't matter. But Lord, hit pleasures us to think now you've done straightened out them legs and that pore bent back and them hands. Hit pleasures us to think on him, movin' around as easy as ary one. And Lord, give him a few red-birds and mebbe a squirrel and a 'coon and a 'possum to keep him comp'ny, like he had here. All of us is somehow lonesome, and we know he'll not be lonesome, do he have them leetle wild things around him, if it ain't asking too much to put a few varmints in Heaven. Thy will be done. Amen.

It may be putting it crudely, but I'm sure that if it took varmints in heaven to make Fodder-wing happy, God provided them. This is the most wonderful surprise of God—the resurrection of Christ. And, when we walk through death's dark vale, as we all must walk, God will walk with us. And at every step he will assure us that on the other side of death he will raise us up and we will be "new creatures."

Will you accept God in earnest? He'll surprise you—with the grandest surprise of all.

Prayer: Though we don't understand completely, we trust thee, our Father. In that trust we are confident. Amen.

DESTINY

The Lesson of the Lark

> "They who wait for the Lord . . . shall mount
> up with wings."—Isa. 40:31 RSV

In the first pages of *The Artist* by Jan de Hartog,
Joost is telling of some of the early events that
made him aware of his artistic endowment. "I've
always been an artist," he said. Then he explains.

His mother had a pet lark named Piet. All
Piet did was sit dumbly in a cage over his mother's
piano. He could not sing or he would not; but
when the mother would play the piano, he would
make a few squeaks. These squeaks created a bond
of deep devotion between the lark and Joost's
mother.

At school Joost had been taught a song about
larks in the spring that climbed an invisible ladder
and vanished in the sky. One day, as he was
convalescing from a tonsillectomy, he lay on his

back in the garden gazing at the white clouds floating overhead. He had an incomprehensible urge to go and play among the clouds or send a messenger carrying a secret message from Joost Jansen to God. So he made his decision. He took Piet's cage into the garden.

What important and fascinating word would he say to God? What message would he send on the wings of this lark? To what would God really listen? The memory of the doctor's chair and the terrible agony of the operation were still fresh, but he decided that a silent messenger would be all he could send, and he opened the cage.

Piet didn't understand at first; then he gave a questioning "tweet," and Joost whispered "tonsils." It was the only word he could think of that would tell it all to God.

Piet understood. He gave a breathtaking surge of tremendous power and rose into the sky fluttering wildly, higher and higher. When he had risen higher than the treetops, for the first time in his life, he began to sing more beautifully than any bird Joost had ever heard. He sang as if he had a little silver trumpet that rang out a song of joy and triumph.

Then, when Joost was certain God was listening and waiting for Piet to bring him his message, the song stopped as if it had been throttled. The wings stopped beating, and the bird plummeted to the earth. Joost beheld death for the first time. He sobbed uncontrollably. He wanted to know why. Why had Piet dropped dead while singing so beautifully? The father explained. The bird had spent all its life in a cage. It had never flown and had never sung. When it was set free and started to climb into the clouds and sing, it overexerted itself and broke its heart.

It's a beautiful and moving story—and very suggestive of our own plight. Spiritually, we were made to soar in the clouds and sing joyfully. But we have not used our spiritual wings, and they have grown stiff. We have not sung the "songs of Zion" and our voices crack when we try.

We can soar to the heights though, and we can sing—we were made for it. A little practice would put us in shape—if we could get out of our cages!

Prayer: We want to sing, our Father—and we want to fly. Loose us from the binding fetters of self and give us thy Spirit which sets us free. Amen.

No Time for Baseball

> "Seek ye first the kingdom of God, and his righteousness; and all these things shall be added unto you."—Matt. 6:33 KJV

In Ernest Hemingway's masterpiece, *The Old Man and the Sea,* the old man, Santiago, has gone far out to sea. This is prior to the battle with the big fish which becomes the dramatic struggle of the novel. Yet, the stage is set when the old man has just caught his bait and is ready to be about his main business—fishing. He says, "Now is no time to think of baseball. . . . Now is the time to think of only one thing. That which I was born for. There might be a big one [in] that school."

Such a time must come in the life of each of us. It is no time for baseball. It is time to think of that for which we were born—not the marginal but the focal. Jesus set the stage for us and defined our purpose in his command, "Seek ye first the kingdom of God." On the first page of his book, *The Story of Philosophy*, Will Durant sets our human quest in this perspective: "We want to know that the little things are little, and the big things big, before it is too late; we want to see things now as they will seem forever—'in the light of eternity.' "

This is no time to think of baseball. There are great decisions to be made, great goals to be achieved, great efforts to be put forth, great battles in which to be engaged.

Tragically, most of our lives are spent "thinking of baseball." Our attention is constantly diverted to the marginal and we miss the focal. We get in on a lot of the sideshows, but we miss the main event under the big top.

We hear the promise of Jesus, "Seek ye first the kingdom of God . . . and all these things shall be added unto you." It's a wonderful ideal, we say. Something within us stirs, and we hear, as it were, the beating of a distant drum. We want to rise and march to the sound. But we don't. We remain in our comfortable armchairs, sitting and thinking. But we don't move. We contemplate the ideal. We consider its implications, and we just wait.

The annual conference of one of the great denominations in America was meeting in the capitol city of a state wrought with crises. The city and state were strife ridden. An explosion in human relations was about to be ignited. The bishop of that conference was preaching on some words from Paul in the midst of a storm. He talked about how he had had a longing to see a storm at sea. And then, in what he presented as a humorous note, he told of how, on the occasion when he had an opportunity while crossing the Atlantic, he went to bed and slept through the storm that he longed to witness.

It wasn't funny to me, as it appeared to the speaker and some of the audience. Another storm was close at hand—a far more serious storm than that on the Atlantic. That man—and the church he was leading—was sleeping through it all.

Great issues are abroad in our world today. Some of them are close at hand. Possible nuclear war, population explosion, the revolution of rising expectations, the quest for racial equality—to mention a few.

This is no time for baseball. The main business of life calls us. That for which we were born summons: "Seek ye first the kingdom of God."

Prayer: We have dallied too long, our Father. May we leave our little games and enter the greatest game: living. Amen.

The Mark of the Master

> "Have we not all one father? hath not one God created us?"—Mal. 2:10 KJV

A few years ago a news release from London announced the discovery of a masterpiece in art.

It was a portrait that had been purchased fifty years ago for $25, but now was worth $150,000 or more.

The discovery was made when two art restorers were examining some canvases in the home of Major Hubert Corlette. The painting was a portrait of Rembrandt's wife, Saskia, whom he painted many times. X-ray and ultraviolet tests showed a Rembrandt signature under an overlay of paint in one corner and proved that the canvas itself was at least three hundred years old.

John Corlette, the major's son, said the picture had long been a family joke because his father always insisted it was an undiscovered Rembrandt. The major's wife had bought the painting at a London auction in 1905.

Because the mark of the master was found upon it, the price went from $25 to $150,000. This is illustrative of one of the great problems of life. It is easy to confuse the unreal with the real, the mock with the masterpiece. It was pictured amusingly in a newspaper verse called "Manhattan Makeshifts":

Drenching my bedroom at night, bright beams
   Bathe me in silvery light by the hour;
I look for the moon, and sad it seems,
   It's only the Metropolitan Tower.

I can almost hear, if I close my eyes,
   The distant roll of an ocean swell,
But I know with one glance at the thwarted skies
   It's the roar of the Second Avenue El.

So much of the artificial surrounds us that we have difficulty in selecting the authentic and culling that which is not.

But once we discover the mark of the master upon it—whether it be in art, literature, or music, we are confident of its value.

It is no less true in our daily conduct. Our values, our attitudes, our relationships, our total experience of living should bear the mark of the authentic. In ordering our lives we should seek for and appropriate that which bears the mark of the Master, Christ.

Prayer: O God, may our lives bear the mark of the Master. May there be no sham and pretense, but only the genuine and authentic. Amen.

For the Sheer Enjoyment of Killing

> "What is man . . . ? Thou hast made him a little lower than the angels, and hast crowned him with glory and honour."—Ps. 8:4, 5 KJV

Consider this scene from a modern novel, *Rampage*, by Alan Caillou. The setting is the Malayan jungle. The characters are Otto von Abart and Harry Stanton, rival big game hunters. The prey: a killer leopard . . . and an even more dangerous woman. Listen to the conversation.

"This is a leopard, Harry. . . . He'll keep close to us just in case he can make a kill. It's the only other animal that kills for the fun of it, and a little group like this will be too much for him to resist."

Stanton raised his eyebrows. "The only *other* animal?"

Von Abart lifted a didactic finger. . . . "The tiger will kill only when he's hungry, and the rhino only when he's disturbed. The elephant won't harm you unless you're fool enough to get between him and his females, and even the crocodile will let you swim if his larder is full. But the leopard—for the sheer enjoyment of killing, just for the pleasure of it. He kills because he likes it. There's only one other animal that does that, Harry. And that's man."

Not a very high estimate of man is it? How fair is the estimate? Cynics would greet the word with favor. To reflect upon the madness of man that, through the centuries, has pitted him against his fellow, to consider the purposeless folly to which he so often gives himself, to see his apparent passion for destruction in the wild wars of history —all this strengthens the cynic in his assessment of the brutality of man.

An obvious area of concern is the current armaments race in which nations are involved. After Hiroshima *Life* magazine warned editorially that "the thing for us to fear today is not the atom, but the nature of man, lest he lose either his conscience or his humility before the ingenerate mysteries of things." And C. E. Montague as far back as 1922, in his novel *Disenchantment,* declared that mankind was "playing golf across the burned hills of hell." That word might be considered prophecy!

Man is playing golf across the burned hills of hell. But the cynics' estimate of man is not the full estimate. There have been those occasions when man could be compared to the leopard, killing "for the sheer enjoyment of killing." There have been those times, also, when he acted out his full potential as a child of God—"created a little lower than the angels, crowned with glory and honor."

Our hope is that man will become what God intended him to be, that he will awaken to his full potential. Let us heed the word of Edwin Markham.

> We men of Earth have here the stuff
> Of Paradise—we have enough!
> We need no other stones to build
> The Temple of the Unfufilled—
> No other ivory for the doors—
> No other marble for the floors—
> No other cedar for the beam
> And dome of man's immortal dream.
>
> Here on the paths of every-day—
> Here on the common human way
> Is all the stuff the gods would take
> To build a Heaven, to mold and make
> New Edens. Ours the stuff sublime
> To build Eternity in time!
>
> —"Earth Is Enough"

Will we mold our lives after the design of the cynic, or will we know who we really are—creatures in the image of God?

Prayer: Awaken us to who we really are, our Father. That is enough, for then we will be like thee. Amen.

Not Fear—but Love

> "May Christ dwell in your hearts as you have
> faith! May you be so fixed and founded in
> love that you can grasp with all the saints
> what is the meaning of 'the Breadth,' 'the
> Length,' 'the Depth,' and 'the Height,' by
> knowing the love of Christ which surpasses
> all knowledge! May you be filled with the
> entire fulness of God!"—Eph. 3:17-19 Moffatt

In the movie from Norman Mailer's novel *The
Naked and the Dead* there is a moving scene that
challenges the position to which most of us have
succumbed. A young lieutenant, one of the leading
characters, is wounded and dying. Two men, a
Baptist preacher and a wandering Jew, carry him
eighteen miles through the jungle. Because of their
sacrifice the lieutenant lives. He had been the
general's aide and the general sought to instill
his philosophy of war, men, and life into the
young man. The philosophy was simple: "the
power of fear and the fear of power."

In a dramatic moment the lieutenant is re-
covering in the hospital when the general comes
to visit him. He is bolted by the young man's
words: "It wasn't fear, Sir. The spirit of man is
godlike, eternal and indestructible—not fear, Sir,
but love."

Say what you will about man, Wordsworth is
still right,

> There's not a man
> That lives who hath not known his godlike hours.

We have known a lot of ungodlike hours in
this generation. We are knowing them now. We

have made the mad philosophy of the general ours: the power of fear and the fear of power.

We are reaping the harvest of that philosophy. On a world level, on a national level, even on a community and personal level, we are reaping that harvest. We have forgotten what the spirit of man is really like! We have so forgotten that we have lost the image. And we fit ourselves into the perverted pattern, not the destined one. The fear of power and the power of fear have become the keynotes of our actions.

Paul and those who have followed in his steps have proved that we are wrong. In the dingy cell of a moldy prison, Paul envisioned a light shining in the midst of darkness, and he wrote a prayer for the church at Ephesus in which he pleaded "that Christ may dwell in your hearts through faith; that you, being rooted and grounded in love, may have the power to comprehend with all the saints what is the breadth and length and height and depth, and to know the love of Christ which surpasses knowledge, that you may be filled with all the fullness of God" (RSV).

That you, being rooted and grounded in love! See it in only one example from history—the unequaled power of love for moral redemption, Gandhi. Clad only in a diaper-like loin cloth and armed only with the gospel of love and passive resistance, weak in body but bold and courageous in spirit, that little man moved upon the face of the twentieth century to inspire a revolution that led to an entire nation's independence. The same power is being witnessed in the Negro revolution of our time. Not fear, sir, but love!

There is no power equal to this for moral

redemption: vicarious suffering, bearing the sins and wrongs of others, suffering for them, carrying upon our hearts the evils and shortcomings of others, especially those who have sinned against us. This is the supreme height to which the human spirit can rise. It is the most magnificent manifestation of the true spirit of man. *Not the fear of power or the power of fear, but love.* This is our destiny.

Prayer: We hear thy voice, our Savior, "love . . . that you may be children of the Father." May we be confident that perfect love casteth out all fear. Amen.

To Catch the Last of All the Angels

> "They were to seek God, and it might be, touch and find him; though indeed he is not far from each one of us, for in him we live and move, in him we exist."—Acts 1:27 NEB

In a previous meditation reference to blind Robert Russell and his autobiography *To Catch an Angel* has been made. At the close of this moving story he puts man's quest in perspective.

In my life I see the age-old pattern of growth, the pattern of the crab. What I had imagined to be only a metaphor now seems to me to be a truth. My blindness has made me more acutely conscious of the attractions of my old shells, and so the fear of death has driven me through and from them perhaps more swiftly than it does most men. My quest began as the quest of Narcissus —the search for the gaudy vessel of my ego. Gradually

140

it became the quest of the Grail, the chalice containing the secret of Man.

And to seek to possess this is to try to catch the last of all the angels.

This is the angel we all would catch. But she is illusive and we never seem to lay hold of her. Dag Hammarskjöld talked about this illusiveness:

> Summoned
> To carry it,
> Alone
> To assay it,
> Chosen
> To suffer it,
> And free
> To deny it,
> I saw
> For one moment
> The sail
> In the sun storm,
> Far off
> On a wave crest,
> Alone,
> Bearing from land.
>
> For one moment
> I saw.

On occasion we get a glimpse; we hear the rustle of a wing; an unexpressible idea struggles to be verbalized. Yet, the reality is not solid enough to image forth.

In our heart of hearts we know, though. We are creatures of God. This is the "hunger in our maw"; this is the restlessness deep within.

Helen Keller never went to church during her

early childhood. Deaf, dumb, and blind, she had no opportunity to learn the story of God as revealed in Jesus. Then she was taken to Phillips Brooks for religious instruction. The great preacher told her, in the simplest possible language, how God had sent Jesus to show his love, to teach us his will, and to make himself known to men. As she heard this, Miss Keller's face lighted up and she spelled into the hands of her interpreter, "I knew all the time there must be one like that, but didn't know his name."

This is our experience. When we learn that our destiny comes round by Galilee to meet us, the illusive angel of meaning no longer evades us. Our destiny is fixed and known in Jesus Christ.

Prayer: Baffled as we sometimes are, confused as life sometimes is, we find meaning, O Christ, in thee. May that meaning increase as we commit ourselves more completely to thee. Amen.

Here Endeth the First Lesson

> "For we know that if our earthly house of this tabernacle were dissolved, we have a building of God, an house not made with hands, eternal in the heavens."—II Cor. 5:1 KJV

Death. The very word rings with a sound that troubles our ears and makes us uncomfortable. Some find it difficult to use the word even when the fact is inevitable. In conversation with the sick and families of the sick we evade the word as though the very speaking of it carried some ominous power. How unrealistic! Death is such a part of life.

Paul, the champion preacher of the resurrection, stated the Christian hope in words that have provided comfort for many at the door of death. "For we know that if our earthly house of this tabernacle were dissolved, we have a building of God, an house not made with hands, eternal in the heavens." Paul knew, as you and I know, that the storms of life beat upon these frail houses of ours. The gales of disease blow. The storms of life beat upon us and fain would destroy these earthly tabernacles. But how well he knew that this was not the end of things, but the beginning. For "we have a building of God, an house not made with hands, eternal in the heavens." How lifeless is life and with what dreadful fear do we face death without this faith. With this faith death becomes the doorway through which we move to something greater than before.

When Thomas Kelly, the Quaker giant of the inner life, died, Gerald Heard wrote a letter to a mutual friend. He had never met Thomas Kelly, but he knew him as one who had grasped "the adequate life" so he could rejoice.

I was filled with a kind of joy when I read of Thomas Kelly. It was formerly the custom of the Winston Salem Community of Moravians in North Carolina to announce the passing of a member by the playing of three chorales by the church band from the top of the church tower. So I feel I want to sing when I hear of such men emerging. I know it is an outward loss to us—though even directly we may gain more than we lose by their joining the more active side of the communion of saints—but I keep on feeling what it must be for a man as good as he to be able to push aside this fussy veil of the body and look unblinking at the Light.

Heard could write this because Thomas Kelly had found the center of life. Simply, serenely, peacefully, and powerfully he lived in the quiet confidence of one who had God at the helm. When we find this Center and give ourselves to it, the confidence of Paul is ours. Death has no power over us. Its fangs have been pulled and its poisonous venom has been rendered impotent.

If we allow this faith to flood our lives *now*, when our little day is done we can pass on in peace, knowing that all is well.

It was never expressed more beautifully than when Dick Sheppard died. This prophet had been one of the burning lights of the English church. The morning after his death, a London newspaper carried a photograph of the pulpit of St. Martin's, from which he had spoken so often to set Britain aflame. A beam of light shone softly down on the reading desk where the Bible was lying open. In the margin of the picture was printed these words: "Here endeth the first lesson."

That's it! That's death in the Christian sense—it is the end, but only of the *first* lesson. Other lessons are ahead. When life is centered in God, through death we take another step to grow up in his likeness.

Prayer: Here is our destiny, eternal Giver of Life, not fourscore years and ten—nor more, nor less—but life everlasting with thee. Keeping thee at the helm we move on to tomorrow, whatever tomorrow holds. Amen.